The Believer's Roadmap for Life on the Road

Ian Foyn

The Believer's Roadmap for Life on the Road
by Ian Foyn

Printed in the United States of America

ISBN 9781628393002

www.xulonpress.com

Dedication

I would like to thank my Lord and Saviour
Yeshuah Ha Mashiach
For leading me along the Roadmap that He has
given me to follow,
And in so doing, I have learned these princi-
ples, and others, first-hand.
And, the precious Holy Spirit that has never
left me nor forsaken me
All the days of my life – as He promised!
And, my Heavenly Father for giving me the
faith I needed to become His son.
I would also like to thank my precious wife for
her unfailing support,
Her longsuffering and Love that I believe is
supernatural.
I would also like to thank Sylvia for her
patience and understanding,
I would also like to thank the publishers for
taking the 'risk' of handling this work.
And finally I would like to thank you, the
reader, for taking the time to ground
Yourself in the Basic Foundational Principles of
the Word of the Living God.

Prelude

"   .Amen!" He said.
   ..The joy rushed through my body heightening the senses of every nerve in my arms, legs and chest, and my mind swam in the turmoil that was my thoughts. The feeling of humility threatened to drive me to my knees in worship of the Living God. Controlling the emotions and my desire to burst into both praise and exuberant thanks for the privilege I had just experienced, I said with restricted enthusiasm: -

"Welcome to the Family of God – My Brother!"

I could feel the cool draft of a refreshing breeze that contrasted the radiating heat that fell upon us from the canvas roof about ten feet above our heads. The tent had been pitched on a vacant piece of veld across from *Wild Waters* in Boksburg.

As I encouraged him to read the word and pray, his face still 'shone' from the work that the Lord had accomplished in his life.

"Find a vibrant Church to attend and fellowship." I could not suggest he attend **PTM**, even though we could see it across the open industrial plots outside the tent, and across the freeway that separated us from the *old Portuguese hall*. It had the name "Present Truth

Ministries" blazoned over the front of the building. I felt that it was morally wrong to do that as the tent was pitched under the auspices of another Preacher.

He had just finished his heart-stirring Evangelistic message and had encouraged those that had 'never met Jesus' to 'come forward' and he would pray for them. He also asked the 'counsellors' to come and stand behind those that had responded to 'the Call'. I had stood behind this young man. We had then moved to behind and below the speakers to the right of the podium. Standing behind the builder's scaffolding that supported the speakers; we could speak openly and pray freely.

I ran through a brief outline of certain Gospel points:-
"Do you know you're a sinner?". . . "Yes."
". . .Blood of Jesus wash you clean. . .Heaven is a free gift. . .not earned or deserved. . .heart. . .walk in new life. . .do you understand what I have shared with you?"
"Yes, now I do."
We had prayed what is called the 'Sinner's Prayer.'

The change on his face was marked. It was like someone was shining a light on his face – his eyes sparkled. It was glorious! I was not surprised or proud of my efforts. I felt so honoured!

It was about three months, or so, later that I heard that this young man was up to the same tricks that he indulged in before he came to the tent meeting. I was told he had 'back-slidden'. Well, I did not know about that! I had no proof and I was not going to judge on the word of another. But, as I followed the road that the Lord had directed me, I began hearing that other Church Bodies and Ministries were experiencing this phenomenon. They were reporting it in an air of despondency.

I was privileged to sit under some great Teachers of the Word during my journey, not least was a man named **Ron Saxby**. On the roadmap that he had, God had directed him to teach the principles that I examine in this work. At the time we were traveling the same road, **Ron** had to Preach/Teach these principles for months on end. I think it was to get through my 'thick skull' that I was to pass it on, and I was not hearing properly.

I eventually took these principles and taught a family that I had met and had the honour of *leading to the Lord*. For the purpose of this book, I shall call them the *Martin Family*. There was **Dad Martin, Mom Martin, Brother Martin** and two **Sister Martins**.

My roadmap took me away from them, but one day, at a cross road, I met up with them briefly. **Dad Martin** had died suddenly. After being assured that they were "OK" and going on with their life, I moved on.

Years later, I heard that they were all still well and **Brother Martin** was ministering to the youth at a large Ministry on the East Rand of Johannesburg. My heart sang!

Then I considered the Taiwanese to whom I had ministered. One precious lady led Her idol-worshipping family to Jesus and they took their idols outdoors and with their own hands set them alight.

Another couple followed their roadmap to the mission field in communist China. While other families and Saints followed their roadmaps to New Zealand and the Philippines in obedience to the call of the Lord.

In Lesotho we saw the change in the Bible School Students and heard recently that some were in 'the Ministry'. Before leaving on the next leg of our journey, we had the reports from these same Students; that although they were Christians for so many years, they felt that only now they were actually 'Born Again'. They finally knew what it meant!

My heart's desire right now is that you would read this book and absorb, digest, pass on, and teach these same principles.

I met someone one day, while following my roadmap, that explained a truth to me that I am going to share with you.

He said to me: -

"Imagine two Evangelists. Both are able to evangelize for twenty-four years without a break.

The first leads 1,000 people to Jesus every day for the 24 years.

The second leads one person to Jesus and spends the year putting into him all the foundations, teachings, truth and doctrine that he can.

At the end of 24 years, which one would have more 'converts'?"

"Hands-down, the one that lead 1,000 people to the Lord each day!" I thought.

"Work it out!" He said. And walked off.

I worked it out.

The first guy: -

365 ¼ days a year times 24 times 1,000. Eazy! = 8,766,000 Wonderful souls in heaven.

The second guy: -

Year 1 = 2 (Including himself.)
Year 2 = 4 (Remember he is also still working.)
Year 3 = 8
Year 4 = 16
Year 5 = 32
Year 6 = 64
Year 7 = 128
Year 8 = 256
Year 9 = 512
Year 10 = 1,024
Year 11 = 2,048
Year 12 = 4,096
Year 13 = 8,192
Year 14 = 16,384
Year 15 = 32,768
Year 16 = 65,536
Year 17 = 131,072
Year 18 = 262,144
Year 19 = 524,288
Year 20 = 1,048,576
Year 21 = 2,097,152
Year 22 = 4,194,304
Year 23 = 8,388,608
Year 24 = 16,777,216 Disciples doing the 'work of the Ministry daily.'

It spoke volumes to me.

I am still an evangelist by heart, and now, I have added the responsibility of passing on the necessary foundations as well.

Table of Contents

Foreword

As the wife of the author, I feel it is a privilege to write this foreword for his book. We have grown up together as believers in Jesus and walked the same paths for more than 40 years.

There is a lot of stress on "mentoring" today but that is something that was unheard of all those years ago. As we walked along the pathways of our spiritual walk we always seemed to be enrolled in the "schools of hard knocks". Thanks to Ian's zeal for the Lord and his love of reading the Word of God we always seemed to graduate from one school and enroll in another.

We sat under some very anointed teachers of the Word from time to time and Ian soaked up everything he was taught. Together with this and his drive to see people come into the Kingdom of Heaven, he got involved in street evangelism (well, actually, any type of evangelism of which he could be a part). I remember the thrill he got when he led someone to Jesus. He continued in these things for a number of years until he led some very good friends to the Lord.

It was at this point that he started to have home Bible studies with these new converts. His desire to see them grounded in the basic foundation of the Christian faith prompted him to teach the very basics of this book. As the years went by and he shared these with more and more diverse people, he realized that there was so little that the average person knew about the Bible. We are living in a "Post Christian" culture now, where children do not grow up going to "Sunday School", and are bombarded with the teachings of evolution (instead of the truths of creation) in schools. I will never forget, while teaching these Bible studies to small group; how one of the new babes in Christ told Ian that he did not know that God had created the world and mankind. He was 34 years old.

This was an eye opener to say the least and prompted Ian to go off on his "rabbit trails" to explain things that we "oldies in the Lord" take for granted. When you talk to people today about "sin" they automatically think of smoking, drinking and adultery. No one thinks of "sin" as being rejection of Jesus with the result of being separated from the Father.

As I said in the beginning, Ian and I walked the same paths together in our walk with the Lord. We both have the same basic foundation and knowledge of the Word. However, as Ian has said in this book, God takes each of our "same" foundation and builds upon it; adding to our own individual characters and strengths and taking us down the many, many different paths that suit our own individuality. Each one of us in the Body of Christ has a special part to play so that the whole body can function properly.

Even looking at the parallels we find with the Body of Christ (as Paul taught in his revelation of the body of Christ) and the human body. The human body has many basic *ingredients* that are necessary for the operation of every single cell to function properly. For an example a cell in the liver and a cell in the eye both have two very different parts to play; but they both need the same basic things to nourish them and keep them alive. If a poison or any foreign element is introduced into the body, it will attack the foundational ingredients, and thereby destroy part of the body.

So it is with the development of each believer, there has to be a correct starting point which is "Jesus". But from here, as we step onto the pathway of our new life we have to get to know how to correctly choose the right stepping stones. One wrong stone can lead us in a totally wrong direction and away from the narrow path that the Bible speaks about.

In today's world it is even more necessary than ever, that new believers in Christ are well taught, and well-grounded, in the basic foundation of their faith. They need to be equipped to answer questions about what they believe and why. They need a good, true and solid foundation upon which to build the rest of their lives. If any new teaching does not fit on the foundation then it has to be checked out. And most of all today, in this world of compromise and tolerance "of all", we need to have the Word of God as our *plumb line* for discerning the truth from the deceptions that face all of us on a daily basis.

This book of Ian's has been a long time in preparation; but I do believe in the divine timing of our God. If ever there was a time for a book like this to be in abundant supply in every pastor's library, it is NOW! In my opinion every person saying "a sinner's prayer" should either be given one of these to read at home or should be taken and discipled through it.

My Prayer is that this book will become a discipleship tool throughout the Body of Christ, so that we can have disciples, and not just converts.

I am Ian's greatest admirer and his Wife.

Denise Foyn.
2nd August 2013.

Provisos

There are certain English language rules that will be ignored in my book. If you wish to know the full reason[1], read the end note at the end of this book. Simply and shortly, I refuse to honour the enemy of my soul or his lackeys in any way. But the Lord, the Saints, the Angels of God and any God Lover shall receive recognition. **I refer in particular to the use of capitalization on names, titles or references.** This is not done through ignorance, but an act of the will. I have had many 'discussions' (with other well-meaning folk) on the subject and not one of the objections they made have convinced me to view this decision any other way. Even the human servants of the enemy shall be referred to in this fashion, if they are mentioned at all.

All Scriptural Quotations have been taken from the King James Version of the Bible. Some of them have been altered to remove the "thee's" and the "thou's". This I have done myself and for the purpose of making it a little more understandable or applicable to the subject under discussion; but the truth therein would not have been altered.

I do not prescribe to, agree with, or otherwise concern myself with different 'camps' of teaching or doctrine. If a truth is to be found in the writings of a certain 'camp' that enhances, extols or exalts the truth of God's Word, I shall use it to the glory of God. If a Baptist, a Charismatic, a 'Word of Faith' or any other 'camp' expounds a truth and it does not contradict Scripture, but rather explains a Scriptural truth, I would consider its worth and apply it to my 'worldview' if it meets the criteria necessary to be accepted.

I am specifically and purposely writing this book from the standard *Greek* mindset because I am (hopefully) speaking to young believers or people seeking the truth of God (which could be *unsaved* people as well) or Saints that have not yet begun their journey of building their foundation and re-establishing their 'Jewish Roots'. My future **'rabbit trails' book** may be written from the *Hebrew* mindset.

In the study of the Word, and in understanding the Word, unless one knows and understands the importance of Covenant, and the Marriage procedures, in the Hebrew context, all of God's working with us will remain a mystery. Although I do not deal with these subjects in any depth herein, please make it a project to research these subjects. As my lovely wife keeps saying: - "If you do not have the **first 11 chapters of Genesis** and the **importance of the Jews** in the right place (in your worldview), then you will have a warped view of Scripture."

My starting point is the Holy Bible and that is my standard. As any good Believer would know that the Word of God is the final authority in all matters pertaining to life and godliness.

UFOs, ETs, evolution, science, anthropology (the study of humanity), astronomy, and other interesting subjects would be dealt with in the **'Rabbit Trails' book**, although I may touch on some of the subjects in this work; and even they are subject to the searchlight of God's Word.

Nothing in this book is intended to be exhaustive or complete. This is but a starting point for your own personal research and investigation. Add to it and study further as you walk the road according to your own personal 'Roadmap'.

I Need you to Know

Your roadmap may be different to mine and mine may be different to dozens of other readers. It is therefore that I have designed this book as a self-study. By the same token, it can be used in groups and by families. The map may look the same, but each person may be on a different road. Our Heavenly Father is quite capable of keeping 'tabs' on all of His Children. He has proven to be unswervingly faithful to me in my journey.

All He has ever asked of me is my obedience. I have slipped from time to time, but He **never** has! All He asks of <u>you</u> is obedience, He shall always remain faithful!

This is a self-study of the Basic teachings for the Roadmap of life of a young Believer, but has been compiled and presented for the serious-minded Child of God as well.

It is believed that if the foundation of the house be firm, the house shall stand all attacks, both spiritual and physical.

(Luke 6:46–49. *46 And why do you call me; Lord, Lord, and do not the things which I say? 47 Whosoever comes to me, and hears my sayings, and does them, I will show you to whom he is like: 48 He is like a man which built an house, and dug deep, and laid the foundation on a rock: and when the flood arose, the stream beat vehemently upon that house, and could not shake it: for it was founded upon a rock. 49 But he that hears my sayings, and does them not, is like a man that without a foundation built an house upon the earth; against which the stream did beat vehemently, and immediately it fell and the ruin of that house was great.)*

This study is aimed at equipping the 'new-born' Believer for his Christian Walk. It is an exciting Walk and the only one worthy of consideration for the spiritually thirsty. As in life itself; it is a, sort of, On-the-Job-Training experience.

This study could be likened to the starting blocks of a Christian sprint athlete. Please do not misunderstand; I do not advocate that the Christian Walk is a 'sprint', but rather a series of events that make up an athletic meeting of eternal renown. Although it may turn out to be a 'marathon', it certainly is not one single Spiritual Athletic Event. Rather, it is like Events that have eternal rewards that require supernatural efforts expressed in a natural world, in a natural way. Each event is repeated at higher grades in each 'season of life' until one graduates to the 'opens'.

Paul mentions that the athlete must follow disciplines and aim at a specific target (vision & purpose) or find himself rejected from the team:

> (1 Corinthians 9:24 – 27. *24 Know you not that they that run in a race run all, but one receives the prize? So run, that you may obtain. 25 And every man that strives for the mastery is temperate in all things. Now they do it to obtain a corruptible crown; but we an incorruptible. 26 I therefore run, not as uncertainly; so fight I, not as one that beats the air: 27 But I keep under my body, and bring it into subjection: Lest that by any means, when I have preached to others, I find myself to be a castaway.*)

What we have here, in this book, are the basic spiritual shorts, shoes, vest, equipment, etc., to clothe and equip the athlete; from the introduction to the sport, to maturity in the sport.

Read all the Scripture references and do the study slowly and carefully. Expand where necessary and as your experience grows. As you read, have your **Bible**, **this book** and a **notebook** open. Write your own notes and check the Scripture references to see how they apply to the subject being discussed.

Before entering into the study, per sé, I need to direct you to the truth that Jesus came to preach the *Kingdom of Heaven*, not *being born-again* or *being filled with the Holy Spirit* or any other favourite doctrine. This being so, all the teachings herein need to be viewed with the Kingdom of Heaven in mind[2]. Maybe, one can see these teachings as *How to access God's Kingdom.*

All types of folk will be reading this study; from those with great faith to those with *little* faith. To whom do I aim this study? I choose to speak to those with *little* faith because those with 'great' faith can still learn from this study. So I ask you, please understand that if you do not need the encouragement in this book, know that this study is actually for the other guy, the one with 'little' faith.

Although I am dealing ostensibly with the <u>Basic Principles</u>, I have found the need to digress onto some other subjects to 'round-off' your understanding, and thereby preparing you for this wonderful walk with the Lord. These issues are, I feel, important to enhance your grasp of what I am teaching here.

There is yet another consideration I would like to make you aware of, that is the fact that you need to check what I say and make sure that what I say is correct. I realize that you may not know enough, just yet, to confirm or reject what I say, but I would like you to have that frame of mind.

> (1 John 4:1 – 3. *1 Beloved, believe not every spirit, but try the spirits whether they are of God: because many false prophets are gone out into the world. 2 Hereby you know the Spirit of God: Every spirit that confesses that Jesus Christ is come in the flesh is of God: 3 And every spirit that confesses not that Jesus Christ is come in the flesh is not of God: and this is that spirit of antichrist, whereof you have heard that it should come; and even now already is it in the world.*)

If you do question something I say or teach, do not come with the point of view of: - "My church teaches. . ." or "The original Greek or Hebrew says. . ." (no one has met the original Greek or Hebrew) or "I feel. . ." or "I have heard. . ." etc., because these are opinions and could stem from a false understanding based upon previous (erroneous) teaching. I am relying on the pure Word of God, and only coming from that source will convince me otherwise.

> (Act 17:11. *11 These were more noble than those in Thessalonica, in that they received the word with all readiness of mind, and searched the scriptures daily, whether those things were so.*)

I also believe that God is more interested in our **character** than our **comfort**. Many times we face hard situations that God uses to perfect our character, even if the situation causes discomfort (perhaps *because* it causes discomfort). God *will* refine our character, if we are his Children, because we will not be compatible with His Kingdom if our character is 'flawed'. In other words, to reign with Him in His Kingdom, we need His character perfected in us.

These Basic Principles of the Oracles of God can therefore also be called *Basic Principles of the Children of the Kingdom of God.*

No Believer has the right to hide the truth from other Believers *Freely you have received, freely give.* (Matthew 10:8 Heal the sick, cleanse the lepers, raise the dead, cast out devils: freely ye have received, freely give.) Find someone with whom to share these truths.

Finally, this is not an exhaustive study, and as such, I shall not be using all applicable Scriptures possible, or covering all possible points; I shall deal with only those I believe to be pertinent. This study is designed to whet your appetite to 'dig deeper'. Add to it as you study further. Make notes in your notebook for future reference or to remind yourself of a beautiful truth discovered.

Introduction

M y heart's desire is to see the quality of educa-
tion (in the things of the LORD) elevated in the
Body of Christ. I desire to see the youngest Saint in the
position to do, and actually be found doing the *work
of the ministry*. No Saint should keep their knowledge
to themselves; and no leader should prevent any Saint
participating in 'Ministry'. We should be passing
on this knowledge, and enjoy the pleasure of seeing
another Saint mature before our eyes. Finally, I desire
to make the world envious of what the 'Congregation'
has. And, we **do** have a superior lifestyle. Sometimes
we don't even realize it. You are designed to rule
and reign on earth with our Lord Jesus Christ! (See
'What is our Purpose on this Earth' in the first 'Rabbit
Trails' book.)

There is only one place in the Bible that speaks of
Basic Principles. The Bible has many 'principles', e.g.
speech principles, belief principles, symbolic principles, etc.; but it has only <u>one set of *Basic Principles*</u>!

I listened to a preacher one day, Rick Godwin, who
was preaching on a certain subject.

Let us, just as an example, say that he was speaking
on 'Tithing'. He then mentioned that he needed to take

a 'rabbit trail', which was simply a subject that he felt needed to be discussed to add value to his preaching topic. It had a direct bearing on the subject of 'tithing', but was not the thrust of his presentation.

Let us use as an example: - 'First Fruit Sacrifice'.

As with the example of 'tithing', the relevance of the topic 'First Fruit Sacrifice' became clearer as to how it fitted together with 'Tithing', as he discussed the 'Tithing' topic further.

It served to fill in a lot of the spaces in the subject discussed. It proved to be necessary and very useful to the hearer.

I picked up on these 'rabbit trails' and felt that indeed, I needed to follow his example. The problem that arose was that there became so many 'Rabbit Trails' that the book threatened to become an excessively voluminous work. So I thought of putting these 'Rabbit Trails' into a separate work, or two. But some 'Rabbit Trails', I felt could not be avoided, if this work was to be the success that I desired it to be. They are therefore included and marked as such.

The Bible is such an expansive and harmonious Manuscript that to mention every topic one could find within its pages, it would require a rather voluminous document to just list the subjects broached. It would cover such diverse subjects as maths, science, UFOlogy[3], astronomy, witchcraft, Catholicism, logical reasoning, evolution, and even to the refuting of Chinese history. The Bible is even able to divide between your soul and spirit; and even identifying your will and intentions that you hide in your heart.

It is for this reason that I restrict myself to the subject on hand, with as few *rabbit trails* as possible. I hope to give you enough to ensure a firm foundation but not so much that we lose our train of thought.

Hopefully, I have given enough to whet your appetite, and little enough to set you on a quest of discovery to answer the questions raised. As you search, my hope is that you discover the Awe of our Gracious Lord and Saviour. This study is to ground you, the Believer, in the Word of our God, but as we look into the Word of life, we cannot but marvel at the greatness of our benevolent and loving God.

Jesus said: - "Search the Scriptures. . .these are they that speak of me." John 5:39.

The Authority of the Scriptures is not only the 'yardstick' of all matters that pertain to life and godliness; it is in fact unassailable (unbreakable). So many lives have been given in the effort of challenging the truth embodied within its pages, and yet it is still here, standing triumphant! The only ones that have succeeded in doing it despite (disservice) are those confessing to be its believers and its propagators; but inwardly, they are proud, deceitful, evil and stubborn liars, bent on perverting the pure Gospel of grace to deliver their secret agenda and promote "another gospel".

The true *Gospel* is that the Kingdom of God is available to the *Whosoever* that would believe and repent.

The true *Good News* is that any olive branch, cultivated or wild, can be grafted into the true Olive tree, the 'seed of Abraham'.[4]

Prologue

M any teachers of the Bible, both genuine and false, tend to separate, or lose sight of, the importance of the Jewish nation to the _Christian Church_. Whether intended or accidentally, they separate the Jewishness of the Church, and they replace the Jewish nation with the Church. This is not acceptable! The Scripture does say that the Jews have been _blinded_ or that some have been _cut out_ of the "Olive tree" (Romans 11:16–29), but that does not mean that they are forgotten, nor does it mean they have lost their importance to God.

The problem with this misunderstanding is that the Church and the preachers of this theology forget the part played by the nuances, language, customs, history, worldview, principles, etc., that are inherent to the Gospel of our Lord Jesus Christ. Because of this, our understanding of the Bible is coloured by our culture, upbringing or similar considerations. Today, Adonai (the Lord) is restoring this understanding to the Church, and the 'Basic Principles,' therefore, must include this understanding.

Losing sight of our Jewishness is the greatest dis-service that the leaders of the "Church" have imposed on the Body of Christ. Understanding the Hebrew culture and the nuances of its language explains many hard-to-understand Scriptures and sayings of Jesus. To go into the subject of our Jewish heritage would require a book of its own (and there are many good ones available today), so please bear with me as I try to illustrate what I mean in too few words.

The Scripture that says a follower of Jesus must *hate his parents, wife, children, etc.,* (Luke 14:25–27) which can be, and often is, misunderstood. The nuances of the language would indicate, rather, 'place first before' or 'to be more important than' Jesus. So what Jesus is saying is simply, "I must be more important to you than your parents, spouse, children, etc." This, then, does not conflict with our requirement to love one another, or even our enemy. In our list of important priorities, Jesus must be *Number One.*

The knowledge we have of God and about God comes from the Jews. The Bible is Israel-centric or Jerusalem-*centric*, not America-*centric*, China-*centric*, South Africa-*centric*, Rome-*centric*, or any other *-centric*. What I mean by this is that everything is to be seen through the eyes of the Jewish writers and a 'Jewish God.' God chose the Jews as His special people because it suited His needs for presenting His Love Letters— the Holy Bible—to the world. So to fully understand it, you need to *put on Jewish glasses.*

Often we imagine Jesus as a vagabond walking about the dry Israeli landscape with a motley crew of ignorant fishermen and sinners. Jesus was a member of an elite group of handpicked Torah teachers. He wore the same garments and trappings that one would picture a Pharisee wearing. When He was 12 years old, He was astounding the teachers with His understanding of the Scriptures. They (the teachers or *doctors*) would have snapped Him up in order to train Him.

Only scholars of special ability would be asked to enter the 'School of the Torah,' which would end when they were. . .wait for it. . .30 years old. The folk often came to Jesus and said: "Rabbi, please. . ." *Rabbi* means *teacher*. How did they know to call Him Rabbi? Only a Rabbi could be referred to by this title.

The answer, of course, is that He dressed like a Rabbi. He had a following of students, like a Rabbi. Many of the terms and colloquialisms He was using were used by **all** the Rabbis in Israel at that time. It is **because** they understood the things He taught, as a Rabbi, that they tried to kill Jesus regularly.

Please believe me when I say that there are NO contradictions or difficult Scriptures and teachings in the Bible. Our God is truth and infinitely faithful, He has worked out the path to eternity perfectly. We need to trust Him explicitly and obey immediately in all that He says. I encourage you to confirm what I say with Scripture and the Holy Spirit of God.

A quick word on the word *Church;*

The commonly used word *Church* is today understood to mean the building where Christian services, and lately, **any** religious services, are held. Many Preachers and Teachers hold that the Church is the Body of Believers that meet in that building. Both of which I treat with respect to their understanding. Strictly speaking, neither are correct. The word *Church* is not an English word at all, it never existed, it was borrowed from the Germanic "kerk" or "kurk", which was used to describe the meeting place of worship of a pagan[5] cult in that country.

The word for the gathering of God's people used in the Hebrew version of our New Testament Scriptures is 'Synagogue', where it is correctly translated in Revelation 2:9 and 3:9. Every other place that it is translated 'Church' is actually inaccurate. When it pertains to the Body of Believers, the Hebrews called them the Assembly, Congregation, People, Brethren, Host, and of their leaders: Elders and Officers. But mostly, they used the word 'Congregation' when referring to the Believers themselves.

What needs to be understood is that the Olive Tree is a picture of God's chosen remnant (Jeremiah 23:3; Zephaniah 2:9; etc.). In the New Testament, Gentiles are privileged to be added to the Olive Tree by the work of Jesus on the cross (See the whole chapter of Romans 11, but especially verses 17 & 24). This means that the Olive Tree began growing with Adam and continued through Noah, Abraham, Isaac, Jacob, David, and down to Jesus, and has now become our Tree by virtue of us being *grafted in*.

This Olive Tree is now called: the Body of Messiah (Christ) or the Bride of Messiah (Christ) or the Congregation, etc. Therefore, I try not to use the term *Church* but rather I attempt to use the term *Congregation* so that you can get used to it.

End Notes

1   Whenever the satan, demons or false religious
    organizations are referred to, I do not feel that they
    should be dignified with the standard capitaliza-
    tions because they are the enemies of God. And,
    they have no compunction in dragging innocent
    lives to the hell that God made for the devil and
    his angels. These spiritual enemies have no qualms
    in maiming babies; attacking minds and bodies; as
    well as instituting unlawful restrictions on man, as
    they force us into serving their ends and purposes.
    By the same token, I would not honour them by
    belittling them or railing against them. This would
    do nothing but draw attention to them the way
    they desire it.

2   Every doctrine we examine <u>must</u> be understood
    to be *In Jesus*. Doctrine itself can become an idol if
    separated from the *Giver of Life* Himself. The first
    century Church focussed on Peter's 'Gospel' and
    claimed to be based upon the seat of Peter (see
    'The Apostolic Ministry' by Rick Joyner, Pg. 47).
    During the *Reformation*, the epistles of Paul became
    the focus. Today, many Churches focus on a truth
    expounded by John. "The *Gospel of Love* by the
    Apostle of Love" they say. To the extent that they
    have formulated a *Love Only* Gospel.

    We have interpreted the teachings of Jesus
    by the teachings of Peter, Paul, John, and others.
    Conversely, it should be that we interpret Peter's,
    Paul's, John's, and others', and. . .OUR, doctrine, by
    what JESUS taught!

    Jesus was *Kingdom* focussed!

    The teachings herein are to be driven by and
    towards a relationship with JESUS – the Door, the

Bread, and the Water of Life. He IS Life itself. His lovingkindness is true Life itself!

Hebrews 1:12; John 5:36; 2 Corinthians 1:20; Galatians 3:16; etc.

If Jesus is not Lord of <u>ALL</u>, then He is not Lord <u>AT ALL</u>!

3   A modern name given to all pro - UFO subjects or topics. 'UFO' means *Unidentified Flying Objects* and many imply *ETs* (*Extra-Terrestrials*) as well. This is an incorrect assumption. A UFO is just that, an *unidentified flying object*, something flying that you cannot identify. e.g. A car hubcap jarred loose from an accident flies up into the air; you see *it* but not the accident; you can report that you saw a UFO. It does not mean that it has an *ET* present.

4   Genesis 12:3 *And I will bless them that bless you, and curse him that curses you: and in you shall all families of the earth be blessed.*

Romans 11:7 – 12; 16 – 25. *7 What then? Israel has not obtained that which he seeks for; but the election has obtained it, and the rest were blinded 8 (According as it is written, God has given them the spirit of slumber, eyes that they should not see, and ears that they should not hear;) unto this day. 9 And David says, Let their table be made a snare, and a trap, and a stumblingblock, and a recompence unto them: 10 Let their eyes be darkened, that they may not see, and bow down their back always. 11 I say then, Have they stumbled that they should fall? God forbid: but rather through their fall salvation is come unto the Gentiles, for to provoke them to jealousy. 12 Now if the fall of them be the riches of the world, and the diminishing of them the riches of the Gentiles; how much more their fulness? 16 For if the firstfruit be holy, the lump is also holy: and if the root be holy, so are the branches. 17 And if some of the branches be broken off, and you, being a wild olive tree, were grafted in among them, and with them partake of the root and fatness of the olive tree; 18 Boast not against the branches. But if you boast, you bear not the root, but the root you. 19 You will say then, The branches were broken off, that I might be grafted in. 20 Well; because of unbelief they were broken off, and you stand by faith. Be not highminded, but fear: 21 For if God spared not the natural branches, take heed lest he also spare not you. 22 Behold therefore the goodness and severity of God: on them which fell, severity; but toward you, goodness, if you continue in his goodness: otherwise you also shall be cut off. 23 And they also, if they abide not still in unbelief, shall be grafted in: for God is able to graft them in again. 24 For if you were cut out of the olive tree which is wild by nature, and were grafted contrary to nature into a good olive tree: how much more shall these, which be the natural branches, be grafted into their own olive tree? 25 For I would not, brethren, that you should be ignorant of this mystery, lest you should be wise in your own conceits; that blindness in part is happened to Israel, until the fulness of the Gentiles be come in.* (Read the entire chapter for a fuller grasp of the subject.)

Galatians 3:16 *Now to Abraham and his seed were the promises made. He says not, And to seeds, as of many; but as of one, And to thy seed, which is Christ.*

5 The meaning of the word for *pagans* today is not the same as the Biblical meaning of the word *pagans*. The word *pagans* of the Bible indicated non-worshippers of the Jewish God. So it could also be rendered *heathen* or *gentile*. None of which had a 'bad' meaning. After some years, *pagan* and *heathen*, came to mean a godless person or a servant of God's enemy. Today, the word *pagan* means a member of an 'alternative religion' (wikka, satanism, witchcraft, being

politically correct, hinduism, islam, acupuncture, tai kwan do, evolution, judo, and similar religions.) – and by extension, indicating that being family of the ONLY true God and His Messiah is nothing more than another type of *religion*. Paganism today includes all the above-mentioned religions as well as quasi- and pseudo-christianity. Paganistic religions all have one thing in common, the underlying source of its origin.

Chapter 1

Introduction to the Bible

History

The Bible consists of 66 books written by 40 authors. Most of them we know, but there are anonymous writers too. Some of the authors wrote one book, some wrote several. The Bible was written (it is believed) over about 1600 years. The amazing thing is that it has one theme and one purpose, even though most authors did not know each other and did not sit down together and decide on what to write.

The Holy Spirit inspired and directed every word and sentence. They too each had their own roadmaps to follow. There are continual discoveries that are being revealed that display the authorship of the Holy Spirit through His men.

Genesis 1 to Genesis 11, gives the history of the world.

Genesis 12 to the end of the Bible gives the history of God's working with man (through the Jewish nation). The Jews call the Old Testament – the *Tanakh*, which is derived from the Jewish acronym from the first three letters of the main divisions of the Hebrew Bible. *Torah* (the law, Pentateuch), *Nevi'im* (Prophets) and *K'tuvim* (writings), thus - "TaNaKh".

The Pentateuch consists of the first five books of Genesis (written by Moses) and is often called the *Law*. But this is misleading. *Torah* literally means "teaching" or "instruction". The teachings of God do include some items that could be termed *Law*, but it is like saying that a Father is 'discipline'. Yes, a good Godly father will discipline his children, but is that all he will do? Obviously, 'no'! Calling *Torah* 'law' is actually a mistake, as it is only partly true.

These then are the components of the Old Testament (in brief). "Old" is used in the sense of *first* or *initial*, not in the sense of *finished* or *completed*. It is very much a part of the Bible and can never be separated from it.

The *B'rit Hadashah* is the Jewish name for the New Testament.

The Jewish name for our Messiah is: - "*Yeshuah ha Mashiach*". The Greek for "*Mashiach*" is *Christos*, whence comes our word *Christ*. *Jesus* is a bit more complicated. 'Jesus' is a result of translations from more than one language.

In some cases, people's names can be translated into another language, others, the name takes on a different form, and still others have no equivalent version of the name and a name is then be 'chosen' for use.

Examples of what I am saying: -

Using *John* as an example. The Afrikaans or Dutch version would be 'Johan/n'; the Scottish would be 'Ian'; the Welsh would be 'Aron'; the Irish would be 'Sean'; and the Chinese (who have no equivalent name), created a sound that represents this name and it sounds something like 'Ye-haan'. During my time as missionary in Taiwan, I was given a combination of two characters, which meant nothing but sounded similar to 'Ian'. They were: - 'E' and 'An' making up 'Ean' and sounded like 'I-haan'.

The simplest way to explain how the modern name *Jesus*, 'evolved', is to list the progression of changes.

(Hebrew) –   Yeshuah [which is the name I prefer to use and means *I am salvation*].
(Greek) –   Iesous.
(Latin) –   Jesu.
(English) – Jesus.

I shall still use the name *Jesus* in this book as it is the most familiar name to the largest portion of the readers of this book (I would imagine). Also, there is still power in the Name of Jesus as it is the name chosen by most English speaking people of the world. As with Chinese (who have no equivalent name for 'Yeshuah', they chose 'Yesu'), the English have chosen *Jesus* to represent the Son of the Living God. People are still being saved in that Name; delivered and set free, in that Name; and devils and demons flee at that Name. That Name HAS Power! – Because of Whom it represents!

B'rit means *covenant* or *contract*, whereas *testament*, which means *contract*, but mainly in the sense of a *will*. *Hadashah* would mean *new books*. The name then would be *The new books of the contract*, although we translate it

47

as the New Testament. It could also rightly (and more pertinently) be understood as the *updated version of the original contract*.

The Bible NEVER introduces the thought that the Gentiles replace the Jews in Biblical history. This is known as 'replacement theology'. It is unscriptural and a false doctrine.

The Bible NEVER introduces the thought that the Jews are set aside while Adonai establishes a *Church* in Scripture. This is known as 'dispesationalism'. It is unscriptural and a false doctrine.

The Scripture that has been perverted to assume this doctrine is found in Romans 11. The first words in chapter 11 are in the form of a question and an answer: - *"I say then, Has God cast away his people? God forbid."* Paul then goes on to explain that the Jews rejected Jesus to give the Gentiles (that is non-Jews) the opportunity to be saved. But it does not indicate that there were no Jews that would be saved or that the Jews would never return, in fact, verse 24 says that it would be easy for them to be grafted in again; and verse 29 says that God's gifts are without repentance!

This particular Scripture (verse 29) is often used to comfort ourselves when our faith wavers. But it also includes the fact that the special, chosen, position of the Jews was without repentance. How can we misunderstand this Scripture, unless we consciously choose to do so? Instead, God has chosen a vessel to raise His Believers above tribal and cultural barriers. He calls it His *Ecclesia* – His *called-out ones* or in our colloquialism, *the Church – The Congregation*.

The actual understanding of *Church* should be: - *Community, Congregation, Called-out Ones or Ecclesia* [transliterated].

We become *Believers*, and that includes Jew, Gentile, Male, Female, etc., and they make up the *Ecclesia of God*.

(Galatians 3:26 – 28. *26 For you are all the children of God by faith in Christ Jesus. 27 For as many of you as have been baptized into Christ have put on Christ. 28 There is neither Jew nor Greek, there is neither bond nor free, there is neither male nor female: for you are all one in Christ Jesus.*)

The Believers that lived before the time of Jesus looked forward to the coming of Jesus to die upon the cross. The believers that have accepted the Blood sacrifice of Jesus after His resurrection look back to His *first coming* for the same purpose. Both were and are saved by their faith in Jesus and are *Born-again* into God's Ecclesia. The *Ecclesia* therefore has never ceased to exist; it has only grown to include the Gentiles. By saying this, I not only imply, but I am saying outright that. . .there is no Old and New *Testament*, there is only one Covenant and one renewed Covenant (being one book).

The image that illustrates what I am saying here is the Olive Tree of Romans 11.

The Jewishness of the Bible

Why is it important to even consider the Jewishness of the Bible?

There would have to be a reason for the Lord to choose the Jews as His Holy nation. A hint at the **first** reason can be found in the call of Abram.

➤ Abram was called "The Hebrew". The name *Hebrew* means *the crossed-over one* or *the one*

49

that has crossed over to the other side (from the root name *Eber*). The nation that Abram came from was idolatrous and served the enemy (the satan). He crossed over (in obedience) to serve and obey the Lord.

➤ The **second** hint can be found in the fact that Hebrew is at the root of every language on earth (hailing back to the tower of Babel), in one way or another[6].

➤ The **third** hint could be found in fact that the understanding of, and about, God and His working is perfectly described in the structure of the language.

➤ The **fourth** hint could be found in the fact that the Jews epitomizes the rebellious nature of man and therefore makes a perfect (living) illustration of all of mankind.

➤ The **fifth** hint could be found in the fact that the culture of these people could trace the lineage of Mashiach (Christ) from Adam to Jesus as a matter of course (as opposed to a special effort being made to keep such records).

➤ The **sixth** hint could be seen in the fact that these traits have continued from creation to today, in spite of the nation being *strawed* throughout the world and then being *reborn* "in one day" (as prophesied), without losing any of these characteristics.

➤ There are **more** reasons, but these should serve our purpose nicely.

We can, therefore, safely say that we serve a 'Jewish' God. Examples of the importance of understanding things from a Jewish perspective would become clearer when we compare it with the Greek culture, language and thought patterns; which are the general influences that we have in most cultures in the world today.

The Greek sees everything in the 'Form' it takes, whereas the Hebrew sees the 'Function' of the 'thing'.

This chart should express some of these comparisons: -

Greek	Hebrew
Focus of *Form* – 'A hand' has five fingers & nails, etc.	Focus of *Function* – 'A hand' comforts, lifts, holds, etc.
Abstract words are meaningful – Love, the fuzzy feeling for another. (Form)	*Abstract* words are meaningless – Love, the sacrifice I make for another. (Function)
Descriptions become adjectives – Pencil, is yellow and eight inches long. (Form)	*Descriptions* become verbs – Pencil, write and erase words with it. (Function)
Nouns have individual meanings – Ram, is a male sheep. Oak is a type of tree. A Post is round. A Mighty Man is strong. (Form)	*Nouns* may overlap in meaning – Ram, is a Mighty protector. Oak is a Strong tree. A Post is a Supportive unit. A Mighty Man embodies all these attributes. (Function)

Further problems in understanding the proper Jewish context of Scripture is: -

• The fact that the Bible translators had to change the Jewish culture and documents into a language that had none of the nuances or words required to interpret the translation correctly (say, English).

• And then further, we read the English translation and we interpret the English into the nuances and traditions of our particular upbringing (UK, New Zealand, South African or other sub-culture).

e.g.

Hebrew (With its nuances, culture, etc.) → into English (With its different nuances, culture, etc.)

English (With its nuances, traditions, etc.) → into English (NZ) (With its different nuances, traditions, etc.)

Now, an English speaking missionary to say. . .Lesotho, will use the English translation and pass teaching to the Sesotho hearers, who in turn, interpret it according to their nuances and culture. The end result may very well not resemble the original intent of God's heart.

Having a common reference point becomes increasingly vital.

A negative when it comes to the Congregation (Church) not understanding the Jewishness of Christianity and the Bible is found in the fact that the Congregation (Worldwide), (sadly to a large extent) has accepted an anti-Semitic stand[7] and teaching. So much so that they do not even realize that they have it. They also reject this *Jewishness* for fear of (would you believe it?) celebrating the feasts of Israel! Talk about straining a gnat and swallowing a camel! Their hesitancy is also grounded in the fear that they would be *brought under the law again.* The fact that they are missing the point of the issue altogether totally escapes them.

Knowing and understanding the Jewishness of the Bible eliminates 'hard to understand' parts and highlights parts we would normally 'gloss' over. Some things are not even mentioned in the Bible because they were accepted as understood; because the Bible was written in Hebrew to Hebrews, and therefore, we (because of our 'Greek' mindset) miss its implication. Further, and for this very reason, the fact that the Bible is in Hebrew to the Hebrews, they divide the Bible into two *Testaments*; which is as heretical as it can come! The Bible is one book from one God to one people[8]! The *Old* is better rendered: - *First part* and *New* is better rendered: - *Updated Part* and *Testament* is better rendered: - *Contract.*

Contents of the Bible

What I mean here is not what books are available; the Bible index can do that, but rather, I refer to the progression of Bible understanding. A Scripture that has always intrigued me and made me wonder is: -

John 16:12 – 15. *(12 I have yet many things to say unto you, but you cannot bear them now. 13 Howbeit when he, the Spirit of truth, is come, he will guide you into all truth: for he shall not speak of himself; but whatsoever he shall hear, that shall he speak: and he will show you things to come. 14 He shall glorify me: for he shall receive of mine, and shall show it unto you. 15 All things that the Father has are mine: therefore said I, that he shall take of mine, and shall show it unto you.)*

For years the devil, through his puppets, has attacked the integrity and validity of the Word of God in an attempt to give the human mind doubt as to its accuracy, reliability and authorship. And these attacks have not abated; in contradistinction, it has intensified. Yet God's Word is still here and still as accurate as ever. Voltaire predicted that Christianity and the Bible would cease to exist in his lifetime. He is gone and his house is now the home of the Bible printing press in France. In the present day, islam has launched a major offensive against the Bible. Websites on the Internet can be accessed freely where the Bible is being ridiculed and God is being defamed.

So, let us examine some interesting proofs that are available to us today that confirms the integrity of the Word of the Living God. When I read *"he will show you things to come"*, in the above Scripture, I questioned, as would any observant person. . .*"is there some truth that is still hidden and will come to light in these last days?"* Yes, there is! But before we examine these, let us remember that as you follow this roadmap, you will note the harmony of the different authors on the subjects we shall discuss. If the one author mentions holiness, the other authors concur to the extent that it seems that one person was writing the Bible.

A bit of *trivia* (or a rabbit trail within a rabbit trail) is called for here, as I deal with this interesting proof, this trivia will come into play. All the languages West of Israel write their languages from left to right. All the languages East of Israel write their languages from right to left. Hebrew can, for different reasons, be written from the left or from the right. The official method however is right to left.

There is a movie/book available called "The Da Vinci Code." It is a load of fictitious nonsense, but like all fictitious nonsense, there is a grain of truth there somewhere. The truth in the "Da Vinci Code" is that there **is** a code in the Bible. But it is certainly not the code portrayed in the movie/book. No one could have accessed the true code without the use of computers. So this code has only become "*visible*" in recent years. This is where the *trivia* comes in. The code is sometimes found reading left to right and sometimes reading right to left.

How it works is that there are Hebrew words and sentences that can be read by choosing, for this example, seven letter intervals. As we continue the example, we can find spelled out, the word "Torah". (Using what is called: - 'ELS' or "Equidistant Letter Sequences".) This was discovered in both Genesis and Exodus going in the left to right direction. In both Numbers and Deuteronomy it was discovered going in a right to left direction. In Leviticus it was not found, instead, the Name of God was found! What makes this intriguing is that the books run Genesis, Exodus, Leviticus, Numbers and Deuteronomy. Genesis and Exodus pointed to God in Leviticus and Numbers and Deuteronomy do the same.

Taking this further, the infamous 9/11 bombings were found in the Bible too. In the Bible, around Ezekiel 37, the following words/sentences were found at the ELS distances in brackets: -

- ✓ Manhattan (698)
- ✓ World Trade Centre (78)
- ✓ Hijackers (29)
- ✓ Ignite the airliner (267)
- ✓ Jihad (210)
- ✓ And more.

There are 26 different words or phrases found in this area of the Scripture passage to do with this cowardly terrorist attack on innocent lives.

The pure mathematical possibility of this occurring by accident is so astronomical that any sane person must admit that it is impossible. Some may say that it is the Hebrew language that lends itself to this sort of phenomena. The scientists that discovered it thought of that and tried it on other Hebrew books – negative results. How about other "holy" books? Not a prayer!

I believe that this is evidence that only the all-knowing, all-wise God authored the Bible. And, this explained to me what that Scripture verse was saying to us "he will show you things to come". It also means that the Holy Spirit will also show us things futuristic, but I shall deal with that subject another time.

Important to Note:

Genesis 9:16. *16 And the bow shall be in the cloud; and I will look upon it, that I may remember the everlasting covenant[9] between every living creature of all flesh that is upon the earth.*

God is a keeper of covenants! He is FAITHFUL and cannot have His Word 'broken'. This applies to ANY covenant He makes.

"The Bible is the inerrant, holy, truth of God. All attempts to prove otherwise have all met with, not only failure (in all cases), but conversion to the faith (in most cases)."

What is the Bible actually?

Should one ask what the Bible is actually? Would I say it was a *religious book*? Would I say it was *poetry* or *prophecy*? Would I say it was a *set of rules*?

This is actually quite a good question.

In summary, I would call the Bible the *Contract between God and man for the biggest Jewish wedding in existence.*

It is this fact that sets it apart from all religious books, doctrine and dogma. It is also for this reason that Christianity or being a *Believer* cannot be classed as a *religion* in the traditional sense of the word. It is more than a lifestyle and it has no equal or even anything approaching its importance to man.

The Bible is, in fact, a single book with a *Marriage Contract* and an updated *Marriage Contract*. It should NEVER be viewed as two books or two individual parts that make up a religious *manual*. It is a contract in which God (the Bridegroom) explains what He wants His Bride to be and how He wants Her to conduct Herself. This is exactly what ancient Jewish practices consisted of when it came to marriages.

There were seven people involved in a Jewish wedding. These were: - the Father of the Groom, the Father of the Bride, the Groom, the Bride, the Scribe, and two Witnesses. The groom would find his bride and ask his father to arrange the wedding. The Father of the Groom would *choose* the Bride by beginning to arrange the details with the Father of the Bride and eventually, supervise the Groom building the future home for the Bride. The Marriage Contract consisted of five parts which the Scribe would write up on the behalf of the Marriage party.

The first part of the contract consists of the combined family history with anecdotes, including family trees. The second part is a personal and family history of the Bride with family tree and anecdotes. The third part is a personal and family history of the Groom with family tree and anecdotes. The fourth part is a story of how the Bride and Groom met with related anecdotes. The Fifth and final part detailed both the Bride's and the Groom's responsibilities before and after the wedding. This Contract is called the *Katubah.*

When following this Marriage process and comparing it to Scripture, it becomes clear that the Torah or Pentateuch [Greek] (the first five books of the Bible) is the Marriage Contract between God and His Bride. (Although the whole Bible does turn out to be the full *Katubah.*)

Important Standards in Understanding the BIBLE

When you do any Bible study, we MUST do our best to understand what God is saying to us. To avoid any mistakes, we need to do four things: -

1. Read the verses before and after the Scripture to get the context [remember, the Bible was not written with chapters and verses].
2. Allow Scripture to interpret Scripture. (Do not take a Scripture on its own as the full thought God is conveying.)
3. Accept any doctrine only by the witness of two or three.[10] In other words, there must be two or three Scriptures [at least] that say the same thing before it can be accepted[11] as God's thought.
4. In all things pertaining to life and godliness (this applies when identifying false religions as well), start with the Bible.

a. The Bible itself claims to be God's Word.
b. Millions of Children of God claim that it is God's Word.
c. Hundreds of false religions acknowledge it is the Word of God.
d. Scientists of every *discipline* recognize it as God's Word.
e. And even the world system acknowledges (grudgingly) it is God's Word (even if only by their hate for it).

Bible book order – Traditional vs. Hebrew

Old Testament	Tanakh
Genesis	B'resheet (Genesis)
Exodus	Sh'mot (Exodus)
Leviticus	Vayikra (Leviticus)
Numbers	B'midbar (Numbers)
Deuteronomy	D'varim (Deuteronomy)
Joshua	Y'hoshua (Joshua)
Judges	Shof'tim (Judges)
Ruth	Sh'mu'el Alef (1 Samuel)
1 Samuel	Sh'mu'el Bet (2 Samuel)
2 Samuel	M'lakhim Alef (1 Kings)
1 Kings	M'lakhim Bet (2 Kings)
2 Kings	Yesha'yahu (Isaiah)
1 Chronicles	Yirmeyahu (Jeremiah)
2 Chronicles	Yechezk'el (Ezekiel)
Ezra	Hoshea (Hosea)
Nehemiah	Yo'el (Joel)

Esther	'Amos (Amos)
Job	'Ovadyah (Obadiah)
Psalms	Yonah (Jonah)
Proverbs	Mikhal (Micah)
Ecclesiastes	Nachum (Nahum)
Song of Solomon or Canticles	Havakuk (Habakkuk)
Isaiah	Tz'fanyah (Zephaniah)
Jeremiah	Hagai (Haggai)
Lamentations	Z'khayah (Zechariah)
Ezekiel	Mal'akhi (Malachi)
Daniel	Tehillim (Psalms)
Hosea	Mishlei (Proverbs)
Joel	Iyov (Job)
Amos	Shir-HaShirim (Song of Solomon)
Obadiah	Rut (Ruth)
Jonah	Eikhah (Lamentations)
Micah	Kohelet (Ecclesiastes)
Nahum	Ester (Esther)
Habakkuk	Dani'el (Daniel)
Zephaniah	'Ezra (Ezra)
Haggai	Nechemyah (Nehemiah)
Zechariah	Divrei-HaYamim Alef (1 Chronicles)
Malachi	Divrei-HaYamim Bet (2 Chronicles)
New Testament	B'rit Hadashah
Matthew	Mattityahu (Matthew)
Mark	Mark

Luke	Luke
John	Yochanan (John)
Acts	The Acts of the Emissaries of Yeshua Ha Mashiach
Romans	Romans
1 Corinthians	1 Corinthians
2 Corinthians	2 Corinthians
Galatians	Galatians
Ephesians	Ephesians
Philippians	Philippians
Colossians	Colossians
1 Thessalonians	1 Thessalonians
2 Thessalonians	2 Thessalonians
1 Timothy	1 Timothy
2 Timothy	2 Timothy
Titus	Titus
Philemon	Philemon
Hebrews	Messianic Jews (Hebrews)
James	Ya'akov (James)
1 Peter	1 Kefa (1 Peter)
2 Peter	2 Kefa (2 Peter)
1 John	1 Yochanan (1 John)
2 John	2 Yochanan (2 John)
3 John	3 Yochanan (3 John)
Jude	Y'hudah (Jude)
The Revelation	The Revelation of Yeshua ha Mashiach to Yochanan

Rabbit Trail Ends. . .

Chapter End Notes

6   Joseph Free, Archaeology and Bible History
(Wheaton: Scripture Press Publications, 1969);
Grant R. Jeffrey, The Signature of God (Water
Brook Press, 2004).

7   My wife and I had to leave a fellowship in England
because the Pastor and his wife would not even
entertain the thought of a POSSIBLE link of the
Bible to this Jewishness and therefore banned the
subject altogether. It was from them that I gleaned
the insight of the fears I mention here. The pity is
that their heart is truly to follow after the Lord.
And they don't even realize that they have this
evil attitude!

The Jewishness of the Bible does not threaten
the work of Jesus on the cross! It actually gives it
colour and meaning. Paul, in 1 Corinthians 12:12 –
26 and on, speaks of parts of the body and likens
the Ecclesia to this body. The traditional understanding that the Ecclesia has concerning the finished work of Jesus could be the body as we were
to see it physically (using this same analogy). The
Jewishness of the Bible gives us the inner, hidden
parts that are not so easily seen and appreciated,
as Paul alludes to in verses 22 and 23. These parts
are not only necessary, but perhaps have MORE
abundant comeliness (beauty) than the 'seen' parts
(verse 23).

Furthermore, how can we possibly attempt to
understand the Bible without the *Jewish* mindset?

8   God's Chosen people. Those chosen for His purposes, both Jew and Gentile.

9   The Noahic covenant reaffirms the conditions of
life of fallen man as announced by the Adamic

covenant, and institutes the principle of human government to curb the outbreak of sin, since the threat of divine judgement in the form of another flood has been removed. The elements of the covenant are:-

1 Man is made responsible to protect the sanctity of human life by orderly rule over the individual man, even to capital punishment (Genesis 9:5, 6; compare Romans 13:1-7).
2 No additional curse is placed upon the ground, nor is man to fear another universal flood (Genesis 8:21; Genesis 9:11-16).
3 The order of nature is confirmed (Genesis 8:22; Genesis 9:2).
4 The flesh of animals is added to man's diet (Genesis 9:3, 4). Man and all animals were vegetarians prior to the flood (Genesis 1:29, 30).
5 A prophetic declaration is made that the descendants of Canaan, one of Ham's sons, will be servants to their brethren (Genesis 9:25, 26).
6 A prophetic declaration is made that Shem will have a peculiar relation to the Lord (Genesis 9:26, 27). All divine revelation is through Semitic men, and Christ, after the flesh, descends from Shem.
7 A prophetic declaration is made that from Japheth will descend the enlarged races (Genesis 9:27). Government, science, and art is the indisputable record of the exact fulfilment of these declarations.

10 There are false doctrines that have been accepted in the past and are now being rejected based on this premise, which is good!

11 An example is that some false religions teach that the Bible says that one can be 'baptized' for someone else. But this is a misrepresentation of the Scripture **1Corinthians 15:29** [*Else what shall they do which are baptized for the dead, if the dead rise not at all? why are they then baptized for the dead?*]. Paul was using this as an example to illustrate the futility of believing **any** doctrine if the resurrection from the dead was not a reality. His discussion was not on baptism, but on the resurrection. The example he used is now preached by some as doctrine.

Chapter 2

How does the Bible work?

The writers of the Bible wrote each book at a different time and in a different way, sometimes even with parts in a different language (Aramaic)! When the translators came to do their work, they would refer to a certain part of that book. Instead of reading through the whole book to find the place they were referring to, and (intending) to avoid confusion, they arranged the books into CHAPTERS and VERSES.

These were not originally in the Bible texts. Now, when we want to find a Scripture passage, we rely on three things (besides the index in the front of the Bible).

1. The Name of the Book.
2. The Chapter in that Book.
3. The Verse in that Chapter.

We now write a reference as: -

- Book Name (in this case, Hebrews)
- Then a number for the Chapter (in this case, 6)
- Then a second number for the Verse (in this case, 1) – but to avoid being mixed up between the numbers, we put in a colon [:] to separate them.

Sometimes we want to refer to two or more verses. We separate them with either a comma [,] or a semicolon [;] or a hyphen [-] or the words 'to' and 'and'. The numbers expressed are always automatically taken as being *inclusive* in all references written or referred to in this way.
Examples are: -

- Hebrews 6:1
- Hebrews 6:1, 2
- Hebrews 6:1; 6:2
- Hebrews 6:1 - 3
- Hebrews 6:1 to 3
- Hebrews 6:1 and 2

Always, it will be: - Book Chapter: Verse/s.
NOTE: - Although the divisions of chapter and verse are helpful to find a particular Scripture, it tends

to break the flow of the thought or message being written; which, in turn, adds to our misunderstanding of the passage.

An Important Attitude to 'Receiving' the Word

James 1:21 says: - "Wherefore lay apart all filthiness and superfluity (indulgence) of naughtiness, and receive with meekness the engrafted word, which is able to save your souls."

What this means (among other things) is that as we read the Word and/or receive teaching on the Word; and if we accept and believe the Word or teaching to be true and accurate, we need to reject all preconceived ideas or previous teaching on the subject and embrace the 'new' truth. This may require further research or maybe some hard decisions and life changes. As an example, you may have subscribed to an anti-Semitic spirit and you now see God's purposes in the Hebrew people. You need to now change attitudes and practices to avoid the same mistake again.

Some lies that have found their way into the Bible Believer's mind that 'helps'[12] to interpret the Bible are: -

1. Evolution. People try to insert 'millions' of years into the creation account. They question dinosaurs' history or how certain dating methods 'prove' the earth to be a certain age in contradistinction to the Biblical account. Advice: discount it and ignore it, just read the Word as it stands! I shall deal with this subject later and prove evolution's errors.
2. "God helps those that help themselves". This is a quote from a secular *fairy tale*. It has no Biblical

validity and is in direct conflict with the truth of the Bible.

3. Secular Humanism. This is in fact a religious system in which they colour 'satanism' to be more acceptable in appearance. Sin, hell, judgement, accountability, etc., are all topics that are taboo in their vocabulary and lifestyle. This leads to passing the blame for their actions to others and their sin becomes *social problems*. There is more to it but I am loathe to spend too much time on them. There are excellent books on this, and other, religious systems (e.g. Author Walter Martin's books).

4. Socialism. This is akin to Communism and invades, removes, erodes and otherwise robs the individual of their rights and freedoms. They cry out: - "for the greater good" and "rights of others" as a pretext to remove individual freedoms. This includes the legal murder of babies, penalizing honest married couples in favour of homosexual preferences; removing your privacy while crying out: - "we respect your privacy!" Normal, healthy discipline is outlawed by quoting non-existent or remote incidences of abuse, and then proceeds to make you (the innocent) an outlaw. There are excellent books on this, and other, religious systems (e.g. Author Walter Martin's books).

5. Reincarnation. This delusion was well thought out. It is the teaching of a mystical progression of lives that each person, supposedly, goes through until they reach 'perfection' and become, either god, or part of god – and in so doing, completes god – who supposedly, is incomplete without you. No evidence in Scripture is found to even

hint at this farce so they claim it is an *experiential 'belief'*. We now speak, jokingly, of: - "if I come back, I want to be a. . ." or, "I am healthier than I was in a previous life. . ." or some such irresponsible drivel. We are thereby condoning and promoting this nonsense.

There is more to be said on this subject, but this should be a good starting point. We must not allow secular 'worldviews' to influence our reading and understanding of God's Word.

Rabbit Trail Ends. . .

Chapter End Notes

12 Here I need to mention a thing called "a world-view". Everyone has one. This is a set of preconceived ideas that we have. Remember, everything we know has come from an *outside source* of some kind. We are not born with a 'starting–out' worldview. Worldviews could have been educated into us to shape our outlook. They could be things that we have observed, or experienced, that has helped to shape our outlook. Or, it could have come to us in a number of other ways. Let's take for example the Sun. Do we see it as God's gift for sustaining life? Do we see it as an eternal source of energy that has always been there? Do we see it as a god to be worshipped? Do we glibly discount it and say "Who cares? I don't care! It is too much effort to make a decision." Or perhaps a totally different thought.. . .**This** is a *worldview*.

When you look at a glass and say "That glass is half-full!" or "That glass is half-empty!" then that impression stems from your own personal 'worldview'. It influences every decision or choice you make.

Believing there is no God is a learned worldview. *Racial* hatred is a learned worldview. Evolution is a worldview forced on you as a child in school.

The importance of having a good worldview is found in the fact that it will influence how you perceive God, the truth, and even the world you make for yourself. Things like 'evolution' and 'being politically correct' (among others) strive to bend your worldview into rejecting God, Jesus and eternal life. Hopefully, this book will give you a roadmap that will shape a good worldview.

Chapter 3

Why You Need to Learn the Basic Principles

H ere I will establish some reasons for studying the *Basic Principles*. We shall read Hebrews chapter 5 and verses 8 to 14; to get the context, and to find the reason Paul mentions the basic principles.

Hebrews 5:8 – 14. *8 Though Jesus was a Son, yet He learned obedience by the things He suffered; 9 And being made perfectly mature, He became the author of eternal salvation to all them that obey Him; 10 Called of God an high priest after the order of Melchizedek. 11 Of whom we have many things to say, but find it hard to say to you, seeing you are dull of hearing. 12 For when the time came that you ought to be teachers, you have need that one teach you again that which is the first principles of the oracles [words] of God; and you have become such as have need of milk and not strong meat. 13 For every one that uses milk is unskillful in the word of righteousness: for he is a baby. 14 But strong meat belongs to them that are of full age, even who by reason of use have their senses exercised to discern both good and evil.*

V8 Although you are a Child of God, you need to learn obedience. This is done by 'suffering'. What this implies is[13] <u>discipline</u>[14].

V9 You receive eternal life by obedience. This obedience to God is in agreeing with His plan of salvation and results in your obedience to parents, spiritual covering (like a husband, father, etc.), true teacher, policeman, etc., [i.e. <u>God appointed authority</u>[15]] as a lifestyle.

V11 Are you *dull of hearing*? This is not physical, and it is not just hearing. It is understanding, and acting upon, what you hear. Here is an example of *hearing* (doing the will of God!): -

Matthew 21:28 – 32. *28 But what do you think? A [certain] man had two sons; and he came to the first, and said, "son, go work today in my vineyard." 29 He answered and said, "I will not:" but afterward he repented, and went. 30 And the man came to the second son, and said likewise. And he answered and said, "I [go] sir:" and went not. 31 Which of the two did the will of [his] father? They say to Him, "The first". Jesus said to them, "Verily I say to you, That the publicans and the harlots go into the kingdom of God before you. 32 For John came to you in the way of righteousness, and you believed him not: but the publicans and the harlots believed him: and you, when you had seen [it], repented not afterward, that you might believe him.")*

V12 <u>You</u> ought to be teachers. *You* means <u>every</u> Believer, and therefore it includes <u>You</u>, not just the leaders. It is not the leaders' responsibility to make you grow. It is their job to supply good food in a good atmosphere. It is your job to listen, understand and grow. [You can lead a horse to water, but you cannot make it drink!] Also, before you can build a house, you need a foundation. These principles are the foundation stones of your Christian Faith. If you do not know these, you will be tossed this way and that way, not knowing what is the truth.

V12 You need to be weaned off the *milk of the Word* so that you can 'eat' the *meat of the Word*. What is 'milk' and what is 'meat'? It is the same as *how you build your 'house'*! Normally, with all things being equal, you shall learn the *theory* – the Milk – and then you shall be given the opportunity to put it into *practice* – the Meat. (And here, I need to interject that this is perhaps the most important reason for learning these principles – if a house foundation is poor, it will never stand the rigors of life!)

Look at this example: -

Luke 6:46 – 49. "*. . .46 And why do you call Me 'Lord, Lord,' and do not the things which I say? 47 Whosoever comes to Me, and hears My sayings, and does them, I will show you to whom he is like: 48 He is like a man which built an house, and dug deep, and laid the foundation on a rock: and when the flood arose, the stream beat vehemently upon that house, and could not shake it: for it was founded upon a rock. 49 But he that does not, is like a man that without a foundation built an house upon the earth; against which the stream beat vehemently, and immediately it fell; and the ruin of that house was great.*"

V13 & V14 God wants mature Christians, not babies. Being a baby isn't bad, i̲f̲ you're a baby! If a baby is seen sucking a 'dummy', it is 'cute', but a twenty-one year old sucking a 'dummy' is pitiful! And, yes! You can *just float along*, as a Christian. But is God pleased with you? Will He say at the end of your time on earth, "Well done, good and faithful servant"? I think that a̲n̲y̲ clear thinking person wants to please God. How do you do that? Become what God wants you to become (a mature Christian!) – Grow up!

> Romans 8:28 – 30. *28 And we know that all things work together for good to them that love God, to them who are the called according to His purpose. 29 For whom He did foreknow, He did predestinate to be conformed to the image of his Son, that he might be the firstborn among many brethren. 30 Moreover whom he did predestinate, them he also called: and whom he called, them he also justified: and whom he justified, them he also glorified.*

> Romans 12:2. *2 And be not conformed to this world: but you must be transformed by the renewing of your mind, that you may prove what is that good, and acceptable, and perfect, will of God.*

Chapter End Notes

13 Adults, do not think that you love your child by employing *Sloppy Agape*. You are, in most instances God's instrument of discipline. And your 'discipline' might need to take the form of corporal punishment.

   And, you children, don't think that the responsibility is totally on the shoulders of the adults. You will have to answer for your response, or lack of response, to a loving parent's efforts.

14 'Sloppy' has the connotation of being watery. 'Agape' is a Greek word meaning *the sacrificial love of God*. So, the practice of weak discipline in the name of 'love' is only a *cop-out* for not carrying out good godly discipline (which may include 'corporal punishment').

15 I need here, to insert an explanation of the 'Authorities'. It is God Who places governments and those in authority. They are to be honoured and obeyed. When these are obviously corrupt or anti-God, they will still attempt to rule the land for the 'good of all'. We must then use our God-given intelligence and ensure that they are obeyed when that is true. The time they abuse their powers and pass laws that hinder your walk with God, they are then relegated to the *lesser authority* status.

   <u>Why</u>? And <u>What</u> does this mean? To answer, ask this question:

   Who is the greatest 'Authority'? – **God**! (of course) He is to be obeyed first! If the laws are levelled against our obedience to Him, then they are evil and to be refuted.

Chapter 4

The Seven Principles

There are seven BASIC PRINCIPLES, and they are found in the book of Hebrews.

In Hebrews 6 we see the seven principles. Again, the principles are not listed clearly and may not have been written to portray a 'Greek' method of understanding [as I mentioned before]. The Greeks would read, learn and understand by listing the important points and analyze everything.

The Jews, on the other hand would see things in picture form.

The Greeks saw it in an analytical **FORM**.

The Jews saw it in a **FUNCTIONAL** picture.

An example would be the 'hand'. The Greek would analyze it and say 'the hand has hair on the back, nails on the end of each finger, creases at all the joints, and the thumb is used to represent strength, the index finger is used to point direction, and the middle finger is used for. . .and so on.' Whereas the Jew would see the hand as 'an instrument to hold, comfort, caress, lift, defend,. . .and so on.'

For the purpose of our teaching, we are using the Greek method to analyze this Scripture. I do this so that we can follow the flow of the individual thoughts; in order to understand the principles to the extent that we can put them into practice in our daily lives.

> Hebrews 6:1, 2. *1 Therefore leaving the principles of the doctrine of Christ, let us go on unto perfection; not laying again the foundation of repentance from dead works, and faith towards God, 2 Of the doctrine of baptisms, and of laying on of hands, and of resurrection of the dead, and of eternal judgement.*

Read the above Scripture and identify the seven principles for yourself. Do not be concerned about the order of them. If you get them muddled, it is not serious. What **is** important is that you try to identify them on your own. (Maybe I have them muddled?)

1. _____

2. _____

3. _____

4. _____

5. _____

6. _____

7. _____

Only after you have filled in your idea of what the seven principles are, do you carry on to the next page to check your answers.

Check your list against my list of the seven principles.

The seven principles are: -

1. Repentance from dead works.
2. Faith towards God.
3. Doctrine of baptisms.
4. Laying on of hands.
5. Resurrection of the dead.
6. Eternal judgement.
7. Maturing, or Growing, or Going on. . . . .

I will link the principles in twos. [i.e. Principle 1 & Principle 2; Principle 3 & Principle 4; Principle 5 & Principle 6.] We can refer to each pair as the *aspects of the Christian life*.

Principles 1 & 2 are the principles of Salvation.

Principles 3 & 4 are the principles of Faith or Daily Life.

Principles 5 & 6 are the principles of Hope.

Principle 7 is a principle that is not mentioned directly, but embraces them all. We need to grow in all areas of our Christian life; therefore it is linked to them all.

The Principles reveal the Light of God

These principles, when held up to any religion, will cause that religion to either stand or fall. This is because the Light the principles give is Truth, the Truth of God. They will never contradict God's Word nor grieve the Holy Spirit of God. False teachers & cults will fall down in the following main areas (among others) with just a little bit of scrutiny.

If a *religion* claims to be of God, it **_MUST_** meet the following (Biblical) criteria: -

- Believe that the Bible is God's only Holy Authority.
- Believe that the Bible is the Word of God.
- Its beliefs must not contradict the Bible.
- Accept the Bible as the final authority in solving issues.
- The doctrine of the Trinity
- The sovereignty of God
- The Deity/Sonship of Jesus
- Only Jesus' Blood washes sin away
- Jesus is the only source of salvation
- The correct worldview of the Person of the Holy Spirit
- The correct worldview of Eternal life/heaven/hell
- The correct worldview of Angels/demons

These principles will then JUDGE them and see if what they say is from God; or the false teachers and cults could be leading precious souls to an eternity in hell; or maybe their doctrine is just a man–made method of control, which is just as bad.

Please understand that the devil **does not deny** the existence of God!

He must recognize the existence of God for his purpose to succeed! He does not want to overthrow God; he just wants to be identified with God as a god! He wants to share God's throne. Should he come to you and say; "I am the devil, serve me!" You will either flee or attack him.

To avoid this, his strategy becomes one of either: -

- Becoming identified with God (hopefully **as God** – calling the work of the Holy Ghost the work of the devil; and, vice-versa)
- Discrediting God (making you doubt God's Word is true)
- Removing your eyes from God onto <u>anything</u> unimportant (thus making non-entities of vital importance)
- Introducing confusing religions to confuse you into confusing who is God and who is not (confusing? – <u>that's</u> the devil's whole idea)
- Coming as an *angel of light* to lead you *religiously* into error
- Causing division and suspicion in the Congregation[16] and in this way destroying unity (usually by petty means)
- Because this is not a discussion on the work of the enemy, I will refrain from mentioning other strategies. These few are sufficient to make my point

Now, **_You_** need to decide how serious you are in your decision to serve the Lord God Almighty!

On a scale of 1 to 10, where 1 is: - "I don't want to serve Him", and 10 is: - "I have no time for anything or anyone else except Him!" How would you rate your desire to serve God?

Note: - Your **DESIRE**, not your available RESOURCES (time, money, etc.)!

1	2	3	4	5	6	7	8	9	10

Mark a box with an 'X'

What is Sin?

Why would I want to consider the subject of sin?

We deal with this subject simply because, sin separates us from God, and man loves sin. And, today especially, man is pitting his wisdom against God's. The 'politically correct' religion dictates that man does not have 'sin' any more, rather, man has 'a problem', 'an issue', 'a challenge', 'a weakness', 'a disease', or some such watered-down *alternative*. God calls it "SIN".

It was sin that came into the world by disobedience of one man (Adam) and death was the reward of that sin. With the sin and death, came the curse of being an enemy of God. All of which can only be undone by and through the Blood of Jesus, shed on the cross. But natural man loves sin and tries to find a religion that does not want him to give sin up and still promises eternal life or some such *good* reward.

To avoid facing the true issue, man will firstly try to: -

- Justify his actions
- Compare himself to another person (normally a *greater* sinner than he)
- Reason himself out of guilt and accountability
- Play his sin down to the point of being insignificant
- Deceive himself into thinking that:
    - God will not judge him because of His love for us
    - The rest of the world is as bad as he and that we will all wind-up in the same place – heaven – because God is fair and cannot discriminate
    - Man is a sinner and was created that way, thus, there will be no judgement

Secondly, man relies upon the "golden rule" (*do unto others as you desire them to do unto you*), because it comes from the Bible.

The error of this way of thinking is: -

- Man desires works to be acceptable to God in lieu of personal holiness
- Man hopes that his good works will outweigh his bad works in the *judgement day*

But, the *rule* was given to regenerated minds, not sinners; **and** this *rule* was never intended to replace true salvation.

Thirdly, man will run after false religions that will give him a measure of comfort without requiring responsibility and accountability from him. If he can carry-on with *business-as-usual*, and not have to buckle to someone else's will – even if it is God's will – that will suit him.

Fourthly, sin is both: omission <u>and</u> commission; actions <u>and</u> belief systems.

I am going to discuss sin in this section, as well as man's attempts to please God man's way. Both are referred to as "Dead Works".

Romans 3:23. *23 For all have sinned[17], and come short of the glory of God,*

Looking at sins as being: transgression, iniquity, missing the mark, error, trespass, lawlessness, and unbelief, which is all described as *sin*, we could honestly say that sin includes too many variations that make avoiding sin far too difficult to comprehend, let alone achieve!

May I summarise it to make the difficulty complete?

Anything that offends God is sin. Whether it is against God directly, or whether it is against a person, intentionally or unintentionally, whether in a thought or an action.

I hope this gives you the impression that you cannot avoid sinning in some way.

But does "sin" actually affect ME?

Where the Bible says that we are 'born in sin', we need to understand what it means. (Psalms 51:5. *5 Behold I was brought forth in iniquity, and in sin my mother conceived me.*)

The Bible does not insinuate that when you come out of your mother's womb that you are smoking, drinking, swearing and reading pornography! It is also not inferring that you were conceived out of wedlock (whether true or not). The Bible is referring to the principle in Genesis 3 where Adam sinned. The Lord said that he would die if he ate of the 'Tree of the knowledge of good and evil', and he ate, but did not die.

Did God lie?

No Way!

Adam died spiritually, in that: -

God first breathed His life into Adam to give him life [Genesis 2:7 *And the LORD God formed man of the dust of the ground, and breathed into his nostrils the breath of life; and man became a living soul.*].

> ➢ Then because the Living God is a life-giving spirit, and
> ➢ He is also Holy [Leviticus 11:45 *For I am the LORD that brought you up out of the land of Egypt, to be your God: you shall therefore be holy, for I am holy.*]

> ➤ Then it is easy to understand that God's holiness cannot stay where sin is.
>   - And if sin entered Adam
>   - God had to leave because of the sin being present in Adam.
>   - When God leaves so does His life-giving Spirit
>   ❖ Adam dies spiritually.

And. . .his body began the 'dying process' [this includes all things physical degenerating]. Death and decay was brought into the world and now all creatures are born to die, including man. It is part of the curse of sin. When you were born, you were born with a dead spirit within your body, although your body began by growing first, it also began the *dying process*. So you are born with the curse of sin operating in you, thus, you are 'born *in* sin'. The Bible calls this kind of sin *iniquity*.

The Hebrew view of Sin

There are three steps or levels of sin.

- 🍂 The thought, as a bird passing overhead, but not entertained is a *light* sin.
- 🍂 The thought is entertained and the sin progresses to action, which can be repented of and forgiveness comes.
- 🍂 The practice becomes a lifestyle and the rebellion causes the sinner to not even entertain the thought of repentance, searing off his conscience, and gladly indulging in that sin.[17]

Chapter End Notes

16 The Ecclesia Definition: - The present Ecclesia consists of and is exclusively the body of born-again, spirit-filled, Saints of God. The Ecclesia was fully opened to Gentiles at Pentecost (in principle), when the Holy Spirit arrived as a mighty wind and tongues of fire; and filled everyone present (including Jesus' mother Miriam), causing them to speak in an unlearned language (simply referred to as *tongues*) [Acts 2:1 - 40]. The gentiles began to be added in practice in Acts 10:1 - 48.

17 Sin, summary: The literal meaning of the Hebrew & Greek words variously rendered "sin", "sinner", etc., disclose the true nature of sin in its many manifestations.

Sin is: -

Transgression, an overstepping of the law, the divine boundary between good and evil (Psalms 51:1; Rom.2:23);

Iniquity, an act inherently wrong, whether expressly forbidden or not [and could include sin against an innocent causing perpetuation of that iniquity through later generations - becoming 'inherited'] (Romans 1:21-23);

Missing the mark, a failure to meet the divine standard (Romans 3:23);

Error, a departure from right (Romans 1:18; 1 John 3:4);

Trespass, the intrusion of self-will into the sphere of divine authority (Ephesians 2:1);

Lawlessness, or spiritual anarchy (1 Timothy 1:9);

Unbelief, or an insult to the divine veracity (John.16:9).

Sin. . .

Originated with the satan (Isaiah14:12-14);
Entered the world through Adam (Romans 5:12);
Was, and is, universal, except for Jesus Christ alone (Romans 3:23; 1 Peter 2:22);
Incurs the penalty of spiritual and physical death (Genesis 2:17; 3:19; Ezekiel 18:4,20; Romans 6:23);
Has no remedy but in the sacrificial death of Christ (Acts 4:12; Hebrews 9:26) received by faith (Acts 13:38, 39).

Sin may be summarized as threefold:

An act, the violation of, or lack of obedience to, the revealed will of God;
A state, absence of righteousness;
A nature, enmity towards God.

Chapter 5

Repentance from Dead Works

T his is the first principle of all the 'basic principles of the Oracles[19] of God'.

NOTE: -   To say that the first principle (of the seven) is the most important is right in one sense, but wrong in another. It is the most important in that it is the starting point of salvation. And, without salvation, all the other steps are meaningless. But, we can <u>never</u> separate the steps from one another. So this makes them equally important.

e.g. Is an _important man_ on earth classed by what he accomplished on earth, or by his birth? Both are important, but neither are _more_ important than the other. It is _his life_ that makes him _important_.

Conviction

Before we deal with repentance, we need to examine an, often-misidentified topic – conviction.

Conviction is <u>not</u> a punishing revelation of our sin that causes us to squirm in discomfort. Conviction may make us uncomfortable, and it may make us squirm, as we realize that we have grieved the Lord. But, it does <u>not</u> cause pain and suffering, especially if we have already confessed it. <u>That's</u> how the devil works (causing pain and suffering). The Holy Spirit reveals it to our heart, and the purpose of this revelation is so that we will recognize it as sin, and confess it, to 'rid ourselves' of it.

God already knows what we have done; He does not need to be shown our sin. <u>WE</u> need to see it. And when we see our sin, recognize it as sin, and confess it as sin, then, we can be washed by Jesus' blood.

How does conviction come?

- ❖ Reading or hearing God's Word
- ❖ Holy Spirit revelation
- ❖ Wrong attitudes and our way of living begin to *bother* us
- ❖ God revealing His goodness to us
- ❖ Gifts of the Holy Spirit in operation

Now, let us deal with 'Repentance from Dead Works', word by word.

Repentance

Repentance means a decision to change, followed by a corresponding action. It is like a turning around. Imagine walking in one direction and then you stop, turn around and walk back the way you came – that is a good picture of repentance. 'Repentance' is a principle that is a very necessary practice for any form of relationship with God.

Joel 2:14. *14 Who knows if he will return and repent, and leave a blessing behind him; even a meat offering and a drink offering unto the Lord your God?*

Acts 3:19. *19 Repent therefore, and be converted, that your sins may be blotted out, when the times of refreshing shall come from the presence of the Lord;*

Acts 17:30. *30 and the times of this ignorance God winked at; but now commands all men every where to repent:*

Acts 26:20. *20 but shewed first unto them of Damascus, and at Jerusalem, and throughout all the coasts of Judaea, and then to the Gentiles, that they should repent and turn to God, and do works meet (acceptable, demonstrating) for repentance.*

2 Corinthians 7:10. *10 for godly sorrow works repentance to salvation not to be repented of: but the sorrow of the world works death.*

I would like to use the example of Luke 15:11 - 32 to show you the right method of repentance. (Stop reading this book and look up this Scripture and read it for yourself.) N.B. V17 - V21.

- He *comes to himself.* This means that he realizes that his actions are wrong and ruining his life. He is about to die V17.
- He *says to himself.* This means that he clearly decides to make right. V18, V19.
- He *returns. . .says to his father. . . .* This means that he carries out his decision. [Corresponding action.] V20, V21.

Summary of Repentance

Quality Assessment
See, understand, realize,
and reject your present position.

Quality Decision
Decide, plan, and desire
to change your present position.

Quality Action
Execute your plan [without plans to return].

(Note: Nowhere in the Bible does it tell us to ask for forgiveness. God does tell us to forgive so that we will be forgiven, and also, that our prayers will not be hindered. But, God does tell us to repent. And God *automatically* forgives us. God reads our hearts before He *reads* our words. If you repent, it is a heart change. Repent means a quality decision to change.)

[Some practice at looking up Scriptures, and also relating the topic from one Scripture to another: - Mark 6:12; Luke 13:3 - 9; Acts 3:19; Acts 17:30; Acts 26:20; 2 Corinthians 7:8, 9; Revelation 2:5, 16, 21, 22; Revelation 3:3, 19; Matthew 9:13; Luke 15:7; Luke 24:47 (N.B.); Romans 2:1 - 29; 2 Corinthians 7:10; 2 Timothy 2:25, 26; Hebrews 6:1; 2 Peter 3:9; Acts 20:21.)]

How do you Repent?

a) Respond to the conviction of the Lord
b) Recognize sin as sin, as opposed to it being called 'a problem' or 'being human'
c) Confess your sin to the Lord
d) Forsake (turn away from) your sin

e) Rely upon the Holy Spirit to wash you in Jesus' blood
f) Believe that God is true and will keep His Word
g) Accept God's forgiveness by faith
h) Move on with the Lord

Wrong Ideas about Repentance

❖ Conviction always precedes repentance; as opposed to getting caught and being put into a position that necessitates a show of repentance.

❖ Conviction always precedes repentance; as opposed to feeling a bitter condemnation – which is normally a sign that the enemy *has his claws in.*

❖ Worldly sorrow has no place in repentance. Worldly sorrow means that you are sorry you got caught – that is all.

❖ Mental assent is not conviction or repentance. I can mentally or intellectually agree on almost anything (with provisos). That does not require a heart attitude change.

❖ Certain religious attitudes. Some religious organizations require certain procedures (works or sacrifices[20]) and actions before they deem you 'forgiven'. Our Father is not like Nimrod[21] who loves suffering and pain; Our Father loves _us_, that is: people!

❖ It is certainly not reformation (sinners can do that too). Reformation is normally a human decision and is broken almost immediately after being made (like our infamous *new-year's resolutions*).

Fruit of Repentance

When true repentance takes place, the following becomes evident: -

- ❖ A hatred of sin (Ezekiel 36:31 - 33)
- ❖ A turning from sinful practices (Acts 19:17 - 20)
- ❖ A godly sorrow (2 Corinthians 7:9 - 11)
- ❖ Confession of sin (1 John 1:9; Luke 15:21; Luke 18:13, 14)
- ❖ Turning to righteousness (1 Thessalonians 1:9; Colossians 3:1 - 14)
- ❖ Restitution, where possible (Leviticus 6:1 - 7; Luke 19:8)

Results of Genuine Repentance

Clearing of your conscience (2 Corinthians 7:10, 11)

- ❖ Remission and forgiveness of sin (Isaiah 55:7)
- ❖ Refreshing from the Lord (Acts 3:19 - 21)
- ❖ Great joy in heaven with the Lord dancing over you (Zephaniah 3:17; Luke 15:7, 10)

Evidence of being 'Saved'

Matthew 7:16 - 23. (For context see verses 24 – 29 as well) *16 You shall know them by their fruits. Do men gather grapes of thorns, or figs of thistles? 17 Even so every good tree brings forth good fruit; but a corrupt tree brings forth evil fruit. 18 A good tree cannot bring forth evil fruit, neither [can] a corrupt tree bring forth good fruit. 19 Every tree that brings not forth good fruit is hewn (cut) down, and cast into the fire. 20 Wherefore by their fruits you shall know*

them. 21 Not every one that says unto me, Lord,
Lord, shall enter into the kingdom of heaven; but he
that does the will of my Father which is in heaven.
22 Many will say to me in that day, Lord, Lord, have
we not prophesied in your name? and in your name
have cast out devils? and in your name done many
wonderful works? 23 And then will I profess unto
them, I never knew you: depart from me, you that
work iniquity.

These Scriptures indicate that you could examine
someone that claims to be a Believer. In this process,
you could find whether they are true or false. This
comes into play when you are faced with false teachers.
But, I would rather you use this to check your own
spiritual condition before the Lord.

Some of the things to look for to indicate your
spiritual genuineness are as follows: -

- ❖ A desire to know/study the Word of God.
- ❖ A desire to pray/spend time in God's presence.
- ❖ A deep, unexplainable, peace in your heart.
- ❖ An abhorrence of sin.
- ❖ A knowledge in your spirit that you are not the same as you were before.
- ❖ Your value system changes.
- ❖ Sins that did not previously bother you now do.
- ❖ You will not resist the teaching about or by the Holy Spirit.

Dead

'Dead' could mean *deceased* – without life; or it
could mean *ineffective, useless, evil*, etc. – which is also,
without life

Genesis 23:4. *4 I am a stranger and a sojourner with you; give me a possession of a buryingplace with you, that I may bury my dead out of my sight.*

Luke 9:60. *60 Jesus said unto him, "Let the dead bury their dead: but you go and preach the kingdom of God."*

[Practice looking up Scriptures, and also relating the topic from one Scripture to another: - Genesis 20:3; John 11:14; Ephesians 2:1, 5; Colossians 3:3; Hebrews 11:12; Jude 1:12; Revelation 3:1; Revelation 20:13.]

Works

'Works' are actions in any normal sense. But in the Biblical sense, it always has the connotation of intentions, thoughts, faith, attitudes, etc.

1 Peter 2:12. *12 Having your conversation [lifestyle] honest among the Gentiles; that, whereas they speak against you as evildoers, they may by your good works, which they shall behold, glorify God in the day of visitation.*

1 John 3:12. *12 Not as Cain, who was of that wicked one, and slew (killed) his brother. And wherefore slew (killed) he him? Because his own works were evil, and his brother's righteous.*

[Practice looking up Scriptures, and also relating the topic from one Scripture to another: - Exodus 5:13; Exodus 23:24; Exodus 31:4; Psalms 8:6; Psalms 14:1; Psalms 17:4; Psalms 33:4; Psalms 33:15; James 3:13; Revelation 2:19; Revelation 18:6; Revelation 20:13.]

Dead Works

Dead works means doing work that is designed or intended to please God or win God's favour; and in so doing, *win or gain* heaven. Dead works then are <u>any</u> works that do not please God. They are seated in your conscience. If you do a work to salve your conscience, it is a 'dead work'.

'Dead works' could include 'good' works. e.g. Praying, evangelizing, reading the Bible, donating money, fasting, etc. These are sometimes the most confusing. A quick way to help with the confusion would be *Look at the Motive!*

Repentance from Dead Works

'Repentance from Dead Works' then means that we need to decide to stop doing useless or unprofitable works (including sin), and then practice our resolve.

Alternatively, we have *living works*. These may be the same works, but done for a different reason and with a different attitude. Living works are done as a *result* of being a Christian and *already having heaven as a possession*! In other words, doing the works as a praise or thanksgiving for what God has done for you.

It **is** necessary to do living works. In fact, God is going to judge you on your living works to give you your reward. So, you **do** need to please God with your works.

Hebrews 9:14. *14 How much more shall the blood of Christ, who through the eternal Spirit offered Himself without spot to God, purge your conscience from dead works to serve the Living God?*

Luke 18:10-14. *10 Two men went up into the temple to pray; the one a Pharisee, and the other a publican. 11 The Pharisee stood and prayed thus with himself, "God, I thank you, that I am not as other men [are], extortioners, unjust, adulterers, or even as this publican. 12 I fast twice in the week, I give tithes of all that I possess." 13 And the publican, standing afar off, would not lift up so much as [his] eyes unto heaven, but smote upon his breast, saying, "God be merciful to me a sinner." 14 I tell you, this man went down to his house justified [rather] than the other: for every one that exalts himself shall be abased; and he that humbles himself shall be exalted.*

We see here that his *good works* were made *evil* by his attitude.

Isaiah 64:4. *4 But we are all as an unclean thing, and **all**[22] our righteousnesses (righteous acts) are as filthy rags; and we all do fade as a leaf; and our iniquities, like the wind, have taken us away.*

Revelation 22:11. *11 He that is unjust, let him be unjust still: and he which is filthy, let him be filthy still: and he that is righteous, let him be righteous still: and he that is holy[23], let him be holy still.)*

This principle is linked to the second in a way that makes them one. The second principle is *Faith Towards God*. These two together make up our *Salvation Principle*.

Chapter End Notes

19 "Oracle" means 'Word'. But it has the implication of will, teaching, desire, requirement, anointing, principle, command, etc.

20 Some religions require one to hurt themselves or give something up that is naturally theirs or do what is sometimes called 'penance'.

21 Nimrod is a character (a *nephal*) in the Bible who actually reintroduced paganism to the world after the flood. He also loved torturing people and seeing bloodshed. Nimrod was also the forerunner of every male idol in mythology after the flood and his mother/wife was the forerunner of every female idol in mythology after the flood. See an excellent book on this subject, "The Two Babylons" by Alexander Hislop.

22 Emphasis mine.

23 Sanctification, holiness, summary:

1 In both Testaments the same Greek and Hebrew words are rendered by the English words *sanctity* and *holy* in their various grammatical forms. The one uniform meaning is to 'be set apart for God'.

2 In both Testaments the words are used of things and persons.

3 When *sanctification* is used of things, no moral quality is implied; they are sanctified or made holy because they are set apart for God.

4 When *sanctification* is used of persons, it has a threefold meaning:

A In <u>position</u>, believers are eternally set apart for God by redemption, "through the offering of the body of Jesus Christ once" (Hebrews

10:10). Positionally, therefore, believers are *Saints* and *holy* from the moment of believing (Philippians 1:1; Hebrews 3:1).

B In <u>experience</u>, believers are being sanctified by the work of the Holy Spirit through the Scriptures as we train our minds, [our souls] (John 17:17; 2 Corinthians 3:18; Ephesians 5:25, 26; 1 Thessalonians 5:23, 24).

C In <u>completion</u>, believers' complete bodily sanctification awaits the appearing of the Lord (Ephesians 5:27; 1 John 3:2).

Chapter 6

Faith Towards God

Let us consider Faith Towards God, word by word.

Faith

This *faith* means *trusting, having faith in* [faith[24] that is *active* and faith that is a *belief system*], *relying on, confidence in,* and *conviction in.* The source of Biblical faith is the Word of God – exclusively! Without faith, it is impossible to please God, and whatever is not of faith is sin, and the just shall live by faith (Hebrews 11:6; Romans 14:23, Habakkuk 2:4; Romans 1:17). This is what makes faith so important.

Many preachers ridicule *hyper-faith*. Then, they go on to preach what they have just called *hyper-faith* as 'Biblical faith'. Do not be drawn into this prideful[25] practice. Faith is not only right and good, it is necessary for the Christian's walk. Some say that it can be taken to excess. Well, that *could* be true, I guess. But isn't it between that person and the Lord? I have never found in the Scripture any reference where **God said**: - "That is too hard for me! Be reasonable, I can't do that!"

I have found in the Scripture where Jesus was shocked at people's unbelief though (like in Mark 6:6)! Only once was Jesus surprised [positively] at a person's *great* faith, and that was the centurion in Matthew 8:10 and other places (same person). I also find where God asks: - "Is there ANY THING too hard for me?" (Jeremiah 32:27).

One thing I shall concede, a person could ask for something before they are mature enough to handle it, and then the Lord would not give it. As a poor (but very illustrative) example; imagine a five-year-old boy praying and asking for a fast car for his birthday. He may ask in sincerity, but with maturity, it becomes an, obviously, foolish request.

Increasing Faith

Can you increase your faith? – Yes, you can increase your faith.

How do you increase your faith? – Here are some tips on increasing your faith: -

- Settle in your heart that God's Word is true and immutable [unchanging]
- Place yourself in a situation where you can hear God's Word regularly
- Become a hearer and doer of God's Word, not just a hearer
- Exercise your faith, like you would a muscle
- Avoid natural reasoning and philosophising, especially where God's Word is concerned
- Believe God's promises
- Be patient, if you fail now, it is not the end of life. Try again. God is big enough to see you through to success

- Do not pray or expect God to take away problems, expect God to help you through them
- Confess your expectation verbally
- Practice obedience to the Lord
- Find the promise in the Word concerning the subject of your faith. Read it, believe it and speak it
- Fulfil any conditions applicable in the Scripture you are claiming as your own
- Patiently accept God's will and answer to the situation (Sometimes 'no', sometimes 'wait' and sometimes 'yes'.)

Exercising your Faith

I mention in a point above: - 'Exercise your faith, like you would a muscle'. I feel this point needs to be expanded upon just a little.

When you know that what you are asking the Lord is indeed His will, then this is a Scripture you can stand upon without wavering: -

2 Corinthians 1:20 *For all the promises of God in him are yes, and in him Amen, unto the glory of God by us.*

To exercize your faith, you need to consider the following: -

➢ God's Promises

First of all, God makes promises to us in Scripture. Some are specific to the Jews, or Gentiles, or His Family, or to the world or even to His enemies. Sometimes, when we are praying and spending time with our Daddy, He would give us personal promises. Sometimes, from the Word and sometimes, quietly to our spirits (where we know, that we know, that He has promised it, and it is hard to explain). I (personally) have had promises given in visions, in dreams, through words of wisdom and words of knowledge from other Saints, and many other sources.

When we recognize these promises as promises, we must never let them go, rather, we need to pray them into 'reality'. We will know that they are promises to us and they are strictly between us and our God.

➢ God's Will

How do you know when or what is the will of God for us at any given time? As with the promises that our Daddy has given us, which is accompanied by whatever instructions in obedience. Likewise, our Father has given us 'commands' that He expects us to carry out when performing His will.
Like: -

- ✓ Love Him above all.
- ✓ Love one another.
- ✓ Preach the Good news.
- ✓ Lay hands on the sick and heal them.
- ✓ And so on. . .what can be termed *generic works*

When seeking God's will, we often ask, specifically, "what job am I supposed to do?"; "where should I live?"; and so on. . .The answer is eazy, do: -
Wherever and however and whatever you want, as long as you. . .preach the Gospel, lay hands on the sick. . .and so on.

"But what ministry should I go into?" "But should I become a Missionary?" or something similar. The answer?

Do wherever and however and whatever you want, as long as you. . .preach the Gospel, lay hands on the sick. . .and so on.

If God has called you to a particular *Mission*, say. . .establish an orphanage (like George Müller) for example, get on with it! Remember, YOU said that God has given you a "MINISTRY". If He did, you cannot fail! If He has not shown you a specific ministry yet, you need to find out from Him what it is He wants you to do. You do this by spending time with Him.

➤ Your Faith

When you have settled in your heart that you have a promise[26], and you have a call, but you have a situation between you and your goal, then it is time to *Faith it Out.*

This means that you need to apply your great faith to the situation and see the Lord move on your behalf. This means you do not give up until you get your answer.

You could be praying for someone to be healed. You could be trusting God for a Job. You could be trusting God for a baby, or any one of a countless list of potential needs or promises that God could have given you. If your initial prayer does not *manifest* your answer. Then, it is an opportunity to exercize your faith!

➤ Exercize your Faith

To explain what I am saying here, I would think an example could be the best way to illustrate my point.

I have been given a word from the Lord while on the Mission Field in Taiwan. It is simple and eazy to understand. Not so eazy to do though! My Daddy told me that He wanted me to follow Him wherever He led, without knowing where or why. He would tell me to go here or there and I would need to obey and go. So many people did not understand me or my call. Now, I have asked Daddy for some fruit where I am right now. I have been feeling that I am *on a shelf* and dormant.

I have to realize that it is time to 'ramp-up' or 'step-up' my faith and believe for more! I am speaking here of something more than just standing on a street corner and handing out Christian tracts [that may be a starting point]. I have come to the point where I have to *pay a price* to take my next step. I must believe God that I can take the next step and sacrifice whatever is needed to achieve my goal. This *sacrifice* may be a fast or committing time to Him in one way or another.

I do not know if I am capable of taking this big step or even in what direction. I just know that He is able to put something out there for me to walk on as I step out onto nothing. This is what I am talking about when I say *exercising* your faith. I have to be prepared to do whatever it takes to move on to the next step with the Lord. I must be prepared to spend whatever time is needed in God's presence until He gives an answer. When He answers, I must be prepared to GO, DO, BE, whatever He says, immediately.

Towards

Notice that *towards* means *in the direction of*. This removes the idea of <u>our</u> ability (as in looking to see what you can do to improve yourself, etc.). The focus is <u>towards</u> God.

If we focussed on *repentance from*, then we would be concentrating on a negative. Also, we would be relying on an effort on our part. The Bible says that it is by <u>faith</u> that we are saved. Any Effort on our part, to either win favour, or to earn forgiveness, or to gain heaven, is a dead work. And the principle of *Faith Towards God* is the principle that directs our *Repentance from Dead Works* into the giver of Eternal Life. This is the part that makes our Repentance from Dead Works a *positive* principle.

God

"God" here indicates the 'Godhead' – Father, Son & Holy Spirit – with <u>all</u> of God's covenant names. A personal study of God's Names is highly recommended.

Chapter End Notes

24 The 'A' and 'B' type of faith.

25 I believe their motive for this practice is to demon-strate how *clever* they are and how *foolish* other Ministries are. We are not called (as an Ecclesia) to the 'ministry of criticism', but to the ministry of reconciliation {2 Corinthians 5:18 & 19. 18 *And all things are of God, who hath reconciled us to himself by Jesus Christ, and hath given to us the ministry of reconciliation; 19 To wit, that God was in Christ, reconciling the world unto himself, not imputing their trespasses unto them; and hath committed unto us the word of reconciliation.*}. Criticism is actually *judging a person.*

26 **I am using a calling as an example. A calling is simply a job that God has given to you to do. It may be praying for the destiny of your children, or a less glorious job, like starting an 'Assembly'. It may be a Mission field you need to go to, it may be a business that God wants you to use to finance the Gospel. It may be that you need to live a life pleasing to the Lord in the face of terrible perse-cution. Apply what I am saying here in whatever situation you find yourself.**

Chapter 7

Who is God?

G od is a Spirit. John 4:24. 24 *God [is] a Spirit: and they that worship him must worship [him] in spirit and in truth.*

It is He that created everything that exists, except Himself. Colossians 1:16. *16 For by him were all things created, that are in heaven, and that are in earth, visible and invisible, whether [they be] thrones, or dominions, or principalities, or powers: all things were created by him, and for him:* See also Revelation 4:11; 10:6.

He is eternal, self-existing, all powerful, all knowing and present everywhere at any one time (Omnipresent). Revelations 19:6; Genesis 17:1; Zephaniah 3:17; etc. [Zephaniah 3:17. *17 The LORD thy God in the midst of thee [is] mighty; he will save, he will rejoice over thee with joy; he will rest in his love, he will joy over thee with singing.*]

God the Father

God chooses to be known as "The Father", because it is He that is our supply, protection, lover and source of all life. Suffice it to say that God chooses how He desires man to perceive Him. One of the names that God refers to Himself as means the "Breasted-One" [Genesis 17:1], indicating that He 'gives suck' to those that need it. This is a female function and has given rise to the drive of the enemy (through certain feminist movements) to confuse the ignorant as to the role of the man and the role of the woman.

A female can never be the source of life. She can only receive from a man, and by supplying her portion, she produces a finished *product*[27]. It is for this reason that God speaks of a man and wife becoming *one flesh*. This is God's pattern and man (or the enemy) can only try to abuse it to defame and insult the *Lord of Life* Himself.

The reason God chooses to be known as a male figure is found in the understanding of the signs, symbols, pictures and functions of a father; and these God has woven into the pattern, life and spirituality of His chosen people – the Hebrew or Jewish nation. (All the way down to the language, writing, foods, and daily life you will find the hand of God present; both functionally and prophetically (and this has, and shall, never change).)

Some of a father's responsibilities: -

- He is the head of the home.
- He makes all the final decisions regarding the welfare of the whole family.
- He is responsible for the spiritual well-being of the family.
- He chooses his son's bride.
- He teaches his son to prepare a home for his new bride.
- He trains his son in the family business matters & skills.

- He provides all the needs of the family.
- He is the protector of the family.
- He is responsible for the financial well-being of the family.
- He rules with a rod of iron (discipline, restrictions, permissions, etc.)
- He rules in absolute love (comforts, guides, heals, advises, provides profound wisdom, is openly approachable, earns respect, etc.)
- He listens to our ideas, suggestions, complaints, etc., and never holds a grudge.
- He never prefers one child over the other, but recognizes the uniqueness of each.
- He rewards the first-born appropriately.
- He is openly approachable to discuss ideas and personal preferences and makes wise suggestions and judgements.
- He is the legal covering of the family to handle all legal activities.
- He initiates all reconciliation and solves disputes.
- He is designed, *built*, and equipped to accomplish these responsibilities.

I cannot cover all that God embraces as Father here, so when you read the Scriptures that refer to the Father, notice His function as well as why He is being mentioned in that particular Scripture (if different from his function).

The TRINITY

There is a group of *know-it-all* religions that claim that there is no such thing as a *Trinity* because the word "TRINITY" does not appear in the Bible. It is similar to the saying about "throwing the baby out with the bathwater". Like the word "rapture" dealt with else-where in this book, it requires a bit of common-sense research. No-one can deny that 'God' is mentioned in the Bible. No-one can deny that 'The Father' is mentioned in the Bible. No-one can deny that 'Jesus' or 'Son of God' is mentioned in the Bible. No-one can deny that 'The Holy Spirit' is mentioned in the Bible. This is still not the common-sense research yet.

The Trinity is indeed true and cannot be disputed. The research comes in when you have to rely upon a mathematical brain. If God = The Father. And, God = The Son. And, God = The Holy Spirit. Then the answer should be: - God = The Father X The Son X The Holy Spirit! The logical result is 1 X 1 X 1 = 1. This is then a "three in one" answer. Geometrically, it represents a perfect cube rather than a line.

["Triune" is a name that can be applied to our God too. It comes from the Latin "tri" meaning 'three' and "unus", Latin for 'one', thus; three in one.]

When you find a Scripture that tells you that God is The Father and also that God is Jesus as well as that God is the Holy Spirit, it leaves you with the impression that: -
God is. . .

1. The Father.
2. The Son.
3. The Holy Spirit.

The 'Father as God' Scripture.

John 6:46. 46 *Not that any man hath seen the **Father**, save he which is of **God**, he hath seen the **Father**.* John 8:41. 41 *Ye do the deeds of your **father**. Then* *said they to him, We be not born of fornication; we have one **Father**, [even] **God**.*

Here Jesus is saying that God is "the Father" and to be sure this is so, look at the reply of the Jews: "*we have one **Father**, [even] **God***". They would have disputed with Jesus if He had said it and it was not true.

<u>The Son as God Scripture.</u>

Matthew 16:16, 17. *16 And Simon Peter answered and said, You are the Christ, the Son of the living God. 17 And Jesus answered and said unto him, Blessed are you, Simon Barjona: for flesh and blood hath not revealed [it] unto you, but my Father which is in heaven.*

Here Peter states that Jesus is the Son of God – the Messiah, no less. Jesus commends him for hearing the truth from God the Father.

<u>The Holy Spirit as God Scripture.</u>

Acts 5:3, 4. *3 But Peter said, Ananias, why has the satan filled your heart to lie to the **Holy Ghost**, and to keep back [part] of the price of the land? 4 Whiles it remained, was it not your own? and after it was sold, was it not in your own power? why have you conceived this thing in your heart? you have not lied unto men, but unto **God**.*

Here Peter is saying that Ananias has lied to the Holy Ghost. Then to clarify it he says that he has not lied to men. . ."*but unto God*".

Let us see if each of the Godhead is said to be equal to each other. We'll start with The Father and Jesus being one.

John 10:30, 31. *30 I and [my] Father are one. 31 Then the Jews took up stones again to stone him.*

Here is a blatant statement and cannot be misunderstood (unless you were determined to corrupt the Word of God). I have included an 'unnecessary' verse, verse 31, just to show you the reaction of the Jews. They understood what Jesus was saying, for sure!

How about, say, Jesus being one with the Holy Spirit?

Romans 8:11. *11 But if the Spirit of him that raised up Jesus from the dead dwell in you, he that raised up Christ from the dead shall also quicken your mortal bodies by his Spirit that dwells in you.*

Romans 10:9. *9 That if you shall confess with your mouth the Lord Jesus, and shall believe in your heart that God has raised him from the dead, you shall be saved.*

Here we see that it was the Holy Spirit that raised Jesus from the dead – no mistake! There is also a bonus in the second Scripture; it says that God raised Jesus from the dead, showing God and the Holy Spirit to be One – AGAIN!

John 10:17. *17 Therefore does my Father love me, because I lay down my life, that I might take it again.*

Here Jesus says that it is <u>He</u> that will *"take it again"* which obviously means that He will raise Himself. If the Holy Spirit AND Jesus raise Jesus from the dead, then the Holy Spirit Is Jesus and Jesus Is the Holy Spirit. A few more Scriptures that you may find interesting are: - Acts 3:15; 4:10; 13:30; 17:30, 31; 26:8; Romans 4:24; etc.

Now, let us find a Scripture that links the three, The Father, the Son and the Holy Spirit, together.

Matthew 28:19. *19 You go therefore, and teach all nations, baptizing them in the name of the Father, and of the Son, and of the Holy Ghost:*

I could continue in this vein but I think this more than does justice to the use of the name *Trinity*. Should someone try to demonstrate his wise knowledge of the Scriptures and state that there is no such thing as a *Trinity* because it does not appear in Scripture, just smile and know that he is being foolish.

Romans 1:21, 22. *21 Because that, when they knew God, they glorified [him] not as God, neither were thankful; but became vain in their imaginations, and their foolish heart was darkened. 22 Professing themselves to be wise, they became fools,*

Have you ever heard of the Star Wars Trilogy? This is a series of science fiction movies that form a sequence. They are called a 'trilogy' because there were three movies. Isn't that clever? The word 'trilogy' was coined in deference to the Christian word for God – "Trinity"? The world that promotes lies, poor morals, false religions, etc., do not have any qualms in recognizing the Holy Trinity, but some *religious* people do. "Strange" I think!

Likening the Trinity of God to the trinity of man.

As a man has a body and a soul and a spirit, but is only one man; so God has a body (Jesus), and a soul (the Father), and a spirit (the Holy Spirit), but He is only one God. The function of a body is to legally be on earth. It is when a spirit manifests himself into the physical that fear is created or caused. It is unnatural and unacceptable to the normal human mind. Even our God aligned Himself with this 'law' when He came to earth. He was born of a woman, a virgin, and thus was on earth legally and because man made no contribution in His birth, was sinless.

I could never describe the Trinity sufficiently to give you a clear picture for you to fully understand Him. Perhaps a picture may help just a **little**. Liken God to the word "SPEECH". You would first require what I call *the voice-box*. Then you would require air to carry the message for it to be *speech*. A vacuum will not carry sound. Finally, you would need a message. The voice-box would be God the father, the air is the Holy Spirit and the message is Jesus. Take any one away and speech does not exist, and by the same token, saying that one is more important or superior to the other is ridiculous in the extreme.

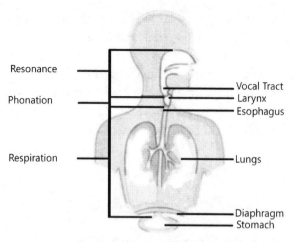

Resonance

Phonation

Respiration

Vocal Tract
Larynx
Esophagus

Lungs

Diaphragm
Stomach

Dynamics of Speech

Understanding God is a matter of getting to know Him, because it is only in the intimate times that He shows you the deeper secrets that are in Him. Speech is not as simple as just a voice-box, a message and air. Believe it or not, you need your skeleton and even your stomach to speak.

There are many body parts that are needed to create speech; but what of the intricacies of the air, and its density or moisture content?

When it comes to the message, it has to be in absolute truth and clear enough for children and adults alike to understand; otherwise it would be a wasted message.

Examining each as an individual component helps to understand its function, make-up and purpose. But we would never separate them for fear of losing 'speech'. This applies to God too. We examine each as an Individual "component" which helps us to understand their function and purpose. But we could never separate them for fear of losing our concept of *the Trinity*. We need to remember, or realize, that the word

Trinity refers to one God, Who has three 'components' (parts), not three 'gods' squeezed into one.

An Almighty, all Powerful, only true God (by nature) would surely be a God that is beyond finite human understanding; that is what would make Him 'God' to us. If He was any less, He would not be that *Awesome, Almighty Being* we call "God".

Rabbit Trail Ends. . .

Faith Towards God

Putting the words "Faith Towards God" all together, we see that we need to rely upon God to get us to heaven. – Jesus paid the price to remove our sin. He rose again to demonstrate absolute victory and to ensure that we receive our inheritance. We need to receive the gift of salvation by receiving Jesus into our hearts (centre of our being/life) and make Him Lord <u>and</u> Saviour of our lives. This is done by faith in God's work (Jesus' efficacious sacrifice), and Word (promise), and absolute integrity; and even **that** faith is not of your own making, it is also a gift of God. So we do not become *good enough*, neither do we first *earn it*, we simply receive it.

Simply stated, *Faith Towards God* is relying on God to make us worthy, righteous, holy, etc.[28] The experience of Noah is a picture of how we must trust God to save us. Noah did not have to swim. He did not have to row the ark. They just rested in God's hands, believing that God would save them.

Genesis 15:6. *6 And he (Abram) believed in the Lord; and it was counted to him for righteousness.*

John 3:18. *18 He that believes on Him is not condemned; but he that believes not is condemned already, because he has not believed on the Name of the only begotten Son of God.*

Related Scriptures: -

Old Testament
Deuteronomy 1:32; Deuteronomy 32:20; Psalms 78:22, 32; Psalms 106:12; Isaiah 53:1; Daniel 6:23.

New Testament
Matthew 6:30; Matthew 8:10, 26; Matthew 9:2, 22, 28, 29; Matthew 15:28; Matthew 18:6; Matthew 21:21, 32; Mark 1:15; Mark 9:23; Mark 11:22 - 24; Mark 16:16, 17; Luke 1:45; Luke 7:9; Luke 8:12, 13, 25; Luke 17:5, 6; Luke 22:32; Luke 24:25; John 3:12, 15, 16, 36; John 4:41; John 5:24, 44, 46, 47; John 6:47; John 7:38, 39; John 8:45, 46; John 9:35 - 38; John 10:26; John 12:36, 38; John 16:9; John 20:29; Acts 5:14; Acts 10:43; Acts 11:21; Acts 16:5,31; Romans 3:28; Romans 4:3,24; Romans 5:1; Romans 14:23; Galatians 3:11, 26; Galatians 5:5, 6; Ephesians 2:8; 1 Timothy 3:9; Hebrews 10:38; 1 John 5:5; Revelation 14:12.

Chapter End Notes

27 The man brings home groceries, the wife produces a meal. The man provides a house, the wife produces a home. The man provides sperm, the wife produces a baby. And so on.

There is a song,"Praise my soul/Indescribable", by *Hillsong United* from their "I stand in awe" album where the man sings the main praise refrain "Praise my soul. . ." and the woman sings of the awesome works and attributes that render the Lord 'Indescribable'. What a beautiful harmony and what an awesome praise song. I think it is one of my *all-time* favourite songs. It also illustrates the man – the covering – and the woman – the harmony – fulfilling their god-given and perfect unity. There is no superiority or subjugation, pride or inferiority. Only two people fulfilling their intended purposes and roles. There is no competition but there is complementation.

28 This is a brief but true story of a man who spanned the Niagara Falls with a cable. He proceeded to call the media (in attendance) and ask if they thought he could cross this cable. Some doubted. So, he proceeded to cross it and return. He then asked if they thought he could do it again, this time pushing a wheelbarrow. Again, some doubted. So, he proceeded to walk there and back pushing the wheelbarrow. He asked if they still doubted whether he could cross pushing the wheelbarrow. This time, there was no doubt. "Then," he said "get in and come with me." He was hard pressed to find someone to accompany him. I tell this story because it is so similar to how we need to trust Jesus to convey us to God's favour.

Chapter 8

Who is Jesus?

B efore answering the above question, I need your opinion: - Who do YOU say Jesus is?

(Tick as many blocks as you wish)

Is He: -

☐ A good man?

☐ A miracle worker?

☐ The Son of God?

☐ A prophet?

☐ A baby in a manger?

☐ A holy man?

☐ Other?

If you answered anything in the vein of Jesus being a good, holy, miracle-working prophet, you are right. We need to see and accept what Jesus says about Himself! Surely Jesus would know Who He is, and I believe we need to see what He has to say. Jesus claims to be a special man, but more than a special man, He claims to be God Himself!

John 8:58. *58 Jesus said unto them, Verily, verily, I say unto you, Before Abraham was,* **I am**.

"Oh but Jesus is not claiming to say He was God" I can hear some say, "You are just reading something into this passage." – I am so glad you mentioned that! The Jews of that time also 'read something' into it, because the Word goes on to say: -

John 8: 59. *59 Then took they up stones to cast at him: but Jesus hid himself, and went out of the temple, going through the midst of them, and so passed by.*

The people would not, in those days, want to stone a man for saying he was a man, but they would if he was blaspheming. But, to fully understand what Jesus was saying, we need to go back to Exodus.

Exodus 3:14. *14 And God said unto Moses, **I AM THAT I AM**: and he said, Thus shall you say unto the children of Israel, **I AM** has sent me unto you.*

Here the God of Abraham, Isaac and Jacob – the God of Creation, is speaking. Jesus is quoting the same words [in John 8] – "ego eimi" [Greek] – that Adonai used, in Genesis 3.

Another very telling passage is found in John 10: 30 – 33.

John 10:30 – 33. *30 I and [my] Father are one. 31 Then the Jews took up stones again to stone him. 32 Jesus answered them, Many good works have I showed you from my Father; for which of those works do you stone me? 33 The Jews answered him, saying, For a good work we stone you not; but for blasphemy; and because that you, being a man, make yourself God.*

(See also: - John 6:35; John 8:12; John 10:9, 11; John 11:25; John 14:6; John 15:1; John 14:1)

It becomes quite clear that Jesus claims, not to be 'a god', but He claims to be **_the_** God of creation! Look at the chart below and make the following decision (You have one of only two alternatives): -

Either He is wrong. . .
or He is right.

If He was Wrong.

You have one of only two choices, if He was wrong: -

Either He **knew** He was wrong. . .or He **did not know** He was wrong.

If He **knew** He was wrong, that would make Him a liar, a deceiver, a hypocrite, a blasphemer, a demon, a fool (he died for it), and a deliberate misrepresenter of God.

You said, previously, that He was a good man, prophet, etc. Would such a man be any of these things (liar, deceiver, etc.)?. . .No?

If He **did not know** He was wrong, that would make Him a lunatic, paranoiac and sincerely deluded.

You said He was a good man, prophet, etc. Would such a man be any of these things (a lunatic, etc.)?. . .No?

Then, surely, He was right. . .He **IS** God!

If He was Right.

But if He **wasn't wrong,** you have one of only two choices: -

You need to either <u>con-sciously</u> and <u>wilfully</u> **reject** Him or <u>consciously</u> and <u>wilfully</u> **accept** Him. If you <u>reject</u> Him, you will <u>face Him</u> as your **Judge**. If you <u>accept</u> Him, you will <u>see Him again</u>, but as your **Lord and King.**

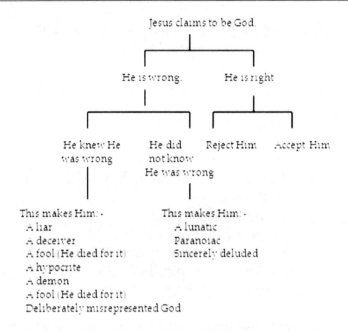

Now remember, you marked the blocks that said that you recognized Him as a 'good man', 'miracle worker', 'Son of God', 'Prophet', 'baby in a manger', 'holy man' or whatever, indicating that He was special – to your mind. Do you think this *special* man could be a liar, lunatic, hypocrite, deluded, demon, etc.? It just does not make sense, does it? He could ONLY be who He claimed to be – God in human form!

I trust that this little exercise has given you a perspective of the seriousness of the claim that Jesus has made. I wonder what decision you have made? Do you accept that Jesus is God or do you reject Him? We are indeed dealing with matters of eternal weight here.

Rabbit Trail Ends. . .

Repentance from Dead Works & Faith Towards God

Putting them both together, we see God's plan of salvation.

When it comes to getting to: -

- Heaven,
- Having a holy relationship with God as your Father,
- Obtaining salvation and,
- Becoming a Child of God then,
  - o It has to be on God's terms. What we find in the Basic Principles **is** God's terms and <u>any other way is false teaching</u>![29]

Some false teachings with another *plan of salvation* are to be found even in *so-called* "Christian Churches". Some believe that baptism will save you, some believe that good works will save you, some believe that 'Church' attendance/registration will save you; but the Bible is explicit. You can only get saved on God's terms.

And that is by. . .'grace – the gift of God'. [Romans 5:15; Ephesians 2:8.]

Without accepting these two principles (Repentance from Dead Works & Faith Towards God), you cannot: -

- Be a Christian
- Be saved
- Go to heaven
- Receive the baptism/indwelling of the Holy Spirit
- Have a personal relationship with God

1 John 5:11-13. Eternal Life is **in** Jesus! If you have Jesus, you have Eternal Life. If you do not have Jesus as a possession, you have **no** Eternal Life! It is as simple as that!

A few considerations: -

➢ You cannot buy any part of Jesus.
➢ You cannot command Jesus to enter or leave another person's life.
➢ You can, further, not demand eternal life without accepting Jesus in all His fullness.
➢ Jesus knows your past, present and future when you accept Him as Lord and Saviour. He still chooses to receive you.
➢ You cannot lose your eternal life by works you do, good or bad, once you have received Him.
➢ You cannot earn God's favour by sacrifice or deeds that may, or may not, please Him.

To become a Christian, get *saved*, or become *born again* (different terms for the same experience) takes a simple[30] prayer. This, or similar, prayer must be said from the heart – i.e. you <u>must</u> mean every word you say. And, you must expect God to respond to your prayer[31].

It is preferable to be with another Christian when you pray this prayer, but it is not a vital necessity. The prayer <u>should</u> be said in your own words. But I have found that many people are not confident enough with their own words and therefore ask to be led in a prayer. With this in mind, I give a sample prayer to guide the one that would like to become a Child of the Living God; but may be hindered by a lack of confidence in praying (there is no shame in lacking confidence, even mature Christians have a lack of confidence at times).

If this is you, do not hesitate to pray (at least) the underlined words in this prayer lesson. In fact, stop and pray it right now. Pray it slowly and thoughtfully. Be aware of what you are saying, and mean it.

The prayer and some explanations run something like this: -

"God in Heaven[32], I come to you in Jesus' name[33].

I acknowledge that I have sinned and deserve to be rejected by You.

I recognize that I have tried to run my life my way – and in so doing, I have failed to please You.

I confess my sinfulness[34] and my inability to correct my own life[35].

I renounce any activity with the occult; I remove any rights or permission that any evil power may think they have over my life.

I reject any curses that may have come from family ties, soul ties, or any other ungodly ties that I may have knowingly or unknowingly allowed into my life.

I cut off any words spoken against me or contracts entered into on my behalf or against me for evil purposes[36].

I reject and renounce any other god that I have served, whether consciously or unconsciously, and I choose to serve You alone.

I ask Jesus to come and live in my heart and wash me in His Blood, making me clean from all my sin. Make my life anew[37].

Holy Spirit, I ask you to write my name in the *Lamb's Book of Life*. Please make me a Child of God.

Father, I receive the honour of the *knowledge of sins forgiven*,[38] and thank You for the fact that I am for-given[39]. I am your Child from this second onwards.[40]

I forgive myself for the many things that I have done that is or would be a source of embarrassment[41].

I thank You, my God, for saving me and I covenant[42] to give thanks to You always for Your goodness.
I also covenant to commit myself to grow in Christ,
and learn more about You, so that I may worship You
in Spirit & in Truth.

I pray this all in the Name of Lord Jesus Christ of
Nazareth[43] – who is now my Lord and Saviour. Amen[44]."

If you prayed this prayer, seriously, I would like to
welcome you to the Body of Christ. You are now my
sibling in Christ. May God bless you!

As I mentioned earlier, the underlined parts of the
above prayer outlines the minimum content of prayer
construction that I would suggest should be used.

Of course, in reality, someone crying "Jesus help!"
in all sincerity would be perfect, in its setting. The story
of an elderly lady, that lived alone and had a visit by
two people, that claimed to represent the satan, may
explain the concept of what I am saying. When this lady
opened her door in response to the knock, the speaker
for the duo introduced themselves as "satanists" going
door-to-door to make their cause known. Her immediate response was to cry out aloud. . ."Jesus help me!"
Both the men fell to the floor and could not rise again.
They eventually crawled away until they were at a 'safe'
distance before they could stand and walk (run?) away.

Getting well-grounded in these principles will
allow you to spot false teaching, help you change, or
encourage you. These are the reasons that God has
given the Basic Principles of the Doctrine of Christ.

"I Prayer that Prayer. . ."

You may ask yourself "How can I be sure God heard
me?" or "How can I be sure that I am now a Child of
God?" [Assuming, of course, that you have prayed the

above prayer in all sincerity. Some have prayed it just to *get someone off their back* and such a prayer is useless.] The answer is, in fact, twofold: -

1. God's promise.

When God makes a promise, you can be assured that it is true and will be carried out! What does God promise?

> John 1:11 – 14. *11 He came unto his own, and his own received him not. 12 But **as many as received him, to them gave he power to become the sons of God, [even] to them that believe on his name**: 13 Which were born, not of blood, nor of the will of the flesh, nor of the will of man, but of God. [Emphasis mine.]*

> John 6:35 – 37. *35 And Jesus said unto them, I am the bread of life: he that cometh to me shall never hunger; and he that believeth on me shall never thirst. 36 But I said unto you, That you also have seen me, and believe not. 37 All that the Father gives me shall come to me; and **him that cometh to me I will in no wise cast out**.*

> Promise   1 Kings 8:56; 2 Chronicles 1:9; Genesis 9:9, 12, 16; Genesis 17:4, 7; Exodus 2:24; Acts 2:39; Galatians 4:28; Ephesians 3:6; 2 Timothy 1:1; **Hebrews 6:17**; **Hebrews 10:36**; Hebrews 11:39; **1 John 2:25**. [Bold references especially pertinent.]

2. By Faith.

We need to mix our faith with God's promise.

Hebrew 4:2 For unto us was the gospel preached, as well as unto them: but the word preached did not *profit them, not **being mixed with faith in them that heard it.*** [Emphasis mine.]

Ephesians 2:8, 9. *8 For **by grace are ye saved through faith;** and that not of yourselves: [it is] the gift of God: 9 Not of works, lest any man should boast.* [Emphasis mine.]

Hebrews 11:6. *6 But without faith [it is] impossible to please [him]: for he that cometh to God must believe that he is, and [that] he is a rewarder of them that diligently seek him.*

Hebrews 13:5, 6. *5 [Let your] conversation [be] without covetousness; [and be] content with such things as ye have: for he hath said, I will never leave thee, nor forsake thee. 6 So that we may boldly say, The Lord [is] my helper, and I will not fear what man shall do unto me.*

By these two immutable (unchanging) things. . . (*Hebrews 6:18. 18 That by two immutable things, in which [it was] impossible for God to lie, we might have a strong consolation, who have fled for refuge to lay hold upon the hope set before us:* Read the 5, or so, verses beforehand to get the context.)

Faith is simply trusting in God's Word, abilities and promises.

What does "Born-Again" mean?

In Genesis we see that Adam sinned and did not die, we also discussed that he had actually died spiritually and the dying process began in nature, from the unseen microbes to the massive stars in space. For us to understand the relationship between body, soul[45] and spirit, I now have to discuss the subject called *the trinity of man.*

What this means is that although man is one composite man, he is made up of three 'parts'. (1 Thessalonians 5:23 *And the very God of peace sanctify you wholly; and I pray God your whole spirit and soul and body be preserved blameless unto the coming of our Lord Jesus Christ.*)

Body   This is the obvious, physical *tent* or *tabernacle* that we live in. This is not the *real* you.

Soul   This 'part of you' is centred in the brain and is the part that contains: -

> ➤ Our Intellect (it is the part we teach and educate)
>   o   Memory
>   o   Mind

> ➤ Our Emotions
>   o   Personality

> ➤ Our Will
>   o   Our Decision-making centre

Spirit   This is the 'part of you' that: -

> ➤ Contains your Character
> ➤ Has the ability to understand God
> ➤ Has the ability to Communicate with God
> ➤ Is 'dead' when you are born into this world
> ➤ Is situated in the middle of your being – or your *heart*. "Heart" here does not refer to the blood pump, but to the middle of your being which is called the *heart* of your being.

When you are born physically, you have a body, a soul and a [dead] spirit (This indicates that you are *born in sin* or born with the *sin-nature*].

When you accept Jesus, He comes into your *heart* (spirit) and gives life to it (1 Corinthians 15: 45 *And so it is written, The first man Adam was made a living soul; the last Adam was made a quickening (life-giving) spirit.*).

It is at this point that you become **Spiritually** 'Born'. This, we refer to as being "Born-Again".

At this point I normally use a hand-drawn depiction of the *trinity of man* and I ask the attendees not to laugh at my drawing attempt. They do always laugh, I do not blame them; and actually, I hope they do laugh. The object of the exercize is not the drawing (good or bad) rather; it is the simple illustration of the subject discussed – and humour is good!

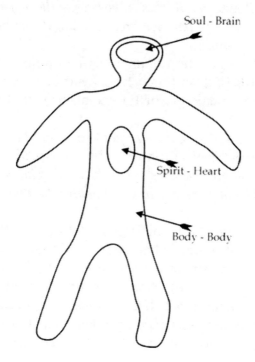

'Born-Again' from a Hebrew mindset

May I give you an example of the depth of meaning of the Hebrew mindset? What I have explained so far – concerning what "Born-Again" means – is absolutely correct. But, when we look at it a little deeper, we find that the Hebrew understanding of creation divides all living creatures into two separate 'lines'.

Line one are those created directly by God, on the one hand; and line two are those created indirectly by God, on the other hand.

In Genesis God created all birds, fish, animals, plants and Adam & Eve. They are all God's ***direct creation***. The ***children of these creations***, whether animal or human, are then an ***indirect creation*** of God.

This is why the Scripture identifies the *Generations of Adam.* (Genesis 5:1 *This is the book of the generations of Adam. In the day that God created man, in the likeness of God made he him;*)

Then we get the *Children of God* or the *Generation of Jesus Christ* [Matthew 1:1]. (Matthew 5:9 *Blessed are the peacemakers: for they shall be called the children of God.*)

As an insult to God, we get those that choose to be *children of the devil.* (1 John 3:10 *In this the children of God are manifest, and the children of the devil: whosoever doeth not righteousness is not of God, neither he that loves not his brother.*)

Finally, we get the defiled line of man by the union of devils and women. The satan tried this tactic to prevent the Messiah from coming to earth (by defiling[46] the lineage of man). And, this union produced the *nephilim.* (Genesis 6:2, 4. *2 That the sons of God saw the daughters of men that they were fair; and they took them wives of all which they chose. 4 There were giants in the earth in those days; and also after that, when the sons of God came in unto the daughters of men, and they bare children to them, the same became mighty men which were of old, men of renown.* [A study of the Hebrew of these verses would reveal the origin of the nephilim.])

We, therefore, that are Children of Adam – and there is nothing wrong with being a son of Adam. This simply indicates that we have the *sin nature* or *unregenerated mind* as the *active nature*. And we are given the awesome privilege of being able to become born directly from God (as Adam was) by becoming "Born-Again". Jesus outlines this experience and opportunity in John chapter 3. Then, in chapter 1 verse 12 John gives us the Evangelist's most powerful promise to the sinner: -

"But as many as received him, to them gave He power to become the sons of God, even to them that believe on His name:"

As we begin to understand the full import of what I have said here, we realize that we are, in fact, taken from the human race (although we still stay in it) and we are placed into, or allowed to enter into, God's heavenly race!

➤ Deuteronomy 14:2 *For you are an holy people unto the LORD your God, and the LORD has chosen you to be a peculiar people unto himself, above all the nations that are upon the earth.;*

➤ Deuteronomy 26:18 *And the LORD has avouched you this day to be his peculiar people, as he has promised you, and that you should keep all his commandments;*

➤ Titus 2:14 *Who gave himself for us, that he might redeem us from all iniquity, and purify unto himself a peculiar people, zealous of good works.*

➤ 1 Peter 2:9 *But you are a chosen generation, a royal priesthood, an holy nation, a peculiar people; that you should show forth the praises of him who has called you out of darkness into his marvellous light:*

Chapter End Notes

29 Many false teachings may sound *good* and *true*, even logical, but the false teaching is normally the *thin edge of the wedge*. The accuracy of the true is to be EXACT or it will lead you incorrectly.

30 Prayer is a Biblical word meaning "communicate with God".

31 The supplied prayer covers most areas that may need to be dealt with in a person's life during their 'conversion'. But folk do not go through the same experiences and thus have differing needs. So, the prayer is to be tailored for the individual praying the prayer. The most important 'requirements' are: -

1 Repentance from all sin (turn away from them).
2 Ask Jesus to become your Lord and Saviour (come into your heart and life).
3 By faith, receive Jesus and receive forgiveness, as well as thanking Him for hearing and accepting you (thankful heart).

32 Many people start praying "Our Father. . ." But how can a non-christian call the Christian God "Father" if He is not his Father? Only born-again Children of God have that privilege.

33 This is the <u>only</u> name by which we can approach a Holy God.

34 Here, many ministers require the person praying to enumerate their specific sins to the Lord. This is good, but often one forgets some of them and later feels that the forgotten sin was not forgiven, and misguided guilt sets in. Also, it could lead to a 'confessional' type situation, which is unacceptable

and unscriptural. When praying and our sins are referred to, it is best to refer to "all" sins, collectively.

35 Acknowledging our sin is stating the truth and agreeing with what God says about us (Romans 3:23; 6:23).

36 This is the part that would set us free from the clutches of the satan and his minions. Some people have never been involved with such activities. Some will deny they were. Some do not recognize what it is and in ignorance will deny it. Some will know that this is them and may even fear the satan and the repercussions for taking such action. Whatever the situation, whether mentioned herein or not, be it known that the Blood of Jesus will set you free and no power of darkness is strong enough to stop you in this action of receiving Jesus as Lord. Also, their power over you will be broken forever – with no further action being able to touch you. Sometimes we do not realize that the satan cannot read your mind and therefore is powerless to stop this process or interfere with this process, but God **can** **read your mind** and answer you.

37 Rejecting this method of salvation is known in the Bible as the 'unforgivable sin' (Matthew 12:31; Mark 3:29; 1 John 5:16).

38 Luke 1:77.

39 This is a faith statement. God has promised that it will happen if you pray this prayer from your heart.

40 Because God's Word says that when I ask Jesus into my heart He will honour that request.

41 This is an action that is as necessary as receiving God's forgiveness.

42 These are statements of commitment. God committed Himself to us; the least we can do is commit ourselves to Him.

43 Do not hesitate to identify the Jesus to whom you are referring. There are many false religions that have a god called 'jesus'. But, it is not the Jesus that you may think it is. When one is coming from that kind of situation, they <u>must not</u> be mistaken and <u>must</u> clearly identify to whom they are speaking.

44 The word 'Amen' means, "so be it" or "I agree" or "Yes", etc. From this, it is obvious that you are saying it as an affirmation that you are happy with what you have just said. Alternatively, the traditional idea that it indicates the end of a prayer is, of course, erroneous.

45 See 'Proof of your Soul' in my 'Rabbit Trails' book (future).

Chapter 9

Doctrine of Baptisms

Read Hebrews 6:1, 2 again. You will notice that there is a plurality of baptisms. But another Scripture says there is only <u>one</u> baptism. It is the same God that requires this baptism.

God is also <u>only one God</u>. In our studying or trying to understand God, we talk about Father, Son and Holy Ghost. We call God "Elohim". *Elohim* has a singular implication but it is a plural word. Similarly, some Greek words for *baptism* have a singular implication but they are plural words.

When it comes to *baptisms* in these spiritual applications, there is only one baptism and cannot be separated {see the comments on Mark 16:16 and Ephesians 4:4-6, below for further expanations}. But, to be able to put this *baptisms* into practice, it needs to be divided up into four different baptisms. These are the four baptisms that every believer will be involved with: -

1. Baptism into the Body of Christ (the Congregation – [Church])
2. Baptism into water

3. Baptism into the Holy Ghost
4. Baptism of suffering

Comments on each: -

Baptism into the Body of Christ (the Congregation)

When you ask Jesus to become your Lord and Saviour, you are automatically put into the True Congregation and given a place, ministry, gift/s, etc., by the Holy Spirit of God. {Notice please, the work is done by the Holy Spirit, that is: - putting the Spirit of Jesus into you.}
What this means in short, is: -

- We are to be holy. We become holy in Jesus. (Leviticus 21:8; Romans 11:16; 1 Peter 1:15, 16; Revelation 22:11.)
- We become one body, in unity and Spirit. (Romans 12:4, 5; Ephesians 2:16; Ephesians 4:4.)
- We become heirs of God. (Romans 8:17; Galatians 3:29.)
- We become Sons of God. (John 1:12; Romans 8:14, 19.)
- We become heavenly people. (Exodus 19:5; Deuteronomy 14:2; 28:18; 1 Corinthians 15:48, 49; Hebrews 3:1.)
- And so on. . .

Ephesians 1:3-7; 10-12; 19-23.

Ephesians 1:3-7. *3 Blessed be the God and Father of our Lord Jesus Christ, who hath blessed us with all spiritual blessings in[47] heavenly places in Christ;*

4 According as he hath chosen us in him before the foundation of the world, that we should be holy and without blame before him in love: 5 Having predestinated us unto the adoption[48] *of children by Jesus Christ to himself, according to the good pleasure of his will, 6 To the praise of the glory of his grace, wherein he hath made us accepted in the beloved. 7 In whom we have redemption through his blood, the forgiveness of sins, according to the riches of his grace;*

Ephesians 1:10-12. *10 That in the dispensation of the fullness of times he might gather together in one all things in Christ, both which are in heaven, and which are on earth; even in him: 11 In whom also we have obtained an inheritance, being predestinated according to the purpose of him who works all things after the counsel of his own will: 12 That we should be to the praise of his glory, who first trusted in Christ.*

Ephesians 1:19-23. *19 And what is the exceeding greatness of his power to us-ward who believe, according to the working of his mighty power, 20 Far above all principality, and power, and might, and dominion, and every name that is named, not only in this world, but also in that which is to come: 22 And has put all things under his feet, and gave him to be the head over all things to the church, 23 Which is his body, the fullness of him that fills all in all.*

➤ God has already blessed us in Jesus (V3)
➤ God has already chosen us to be perfect (V4)
➤ God has already predestinated us to be 'sons' (V5)
➤ We have already been redeemed and our sins forgiven through Jesus (V7)

➤ We already have an inheritance and we are a praise to God in Jesus (V10-12)
➤ God gave His power demonstration by already giving us a part in Jesus when He raised up Jesus from the dead (V19)
➤ God has already set Jesus as head of His body and put the enemy (all enemies of God) under the feet of Jesus (V20, 21)
➤ God has made us part of the Body of Jesus, and made Jesus our head, and the enemy our footstool (V22, 23)

Galatians 4:1, 2. *1 Now I say, That the heir, as long as he is a child, differs nothing from a servant, though he be lord of all; 2 But is under tutors and governors until the time appointed of the father*[49].

Who is this talking about here? Who is "lord of all"? Read Galatians 3: [19 -] 26 - 29, [Galatians 4:1 -7].

• When we are "in Christ", "baptized into Christ", etc., there is no man, woman, Jew, Chinese, black, white, etc., just Christians or Saints or Children of the Living God!
• The obedient Children of Abraham's seed and heirs of God according to God's promise.
• We are the heirs and 'lords of all'!
• Why? We are *in Christ!*

(Galatians 4:9; Proverbs 28:1; Philippians 1:14; 1 Thessalonians 2:2; Ephesians 6:10; Luke 1:74. N.B. Acts 13:24.)

Baptism into water

This is a sign of obedience and commitment by you to all that want to see and know what you believe. You are cut off from contact with the devil [by the Holy Spirit] and he [the devil] has no hold on you any longer. Water baptism is your total, open, and blatant commitment to God. {Please notice; the work is done by the Holy Spirit, that is: – cutting the enemy from you. The water in itself is ineffective in the sense that it has no power to save you; it is the <u>act</u> that is important.} The reason cutting off the enemy's access to you is important is quite self-explanatory. If we allow the enemy to stay too close to us, his influence would tire us and weaken our resolve. Also, with the fact that he wants to identify with the Lord and be identified as a god would become more likely if he is allowed near the Saints for too long a period.

<u>How are you Baptized?</u>

We hear of many people who say that the method of baptism is not important. It is <u>only</u> important that you <u>get baptized</u>. If they were speaking of the place of baptism or the person doing the baptism, then I would tend to agree with them. But, if they are talking about the actual symbol, then I am forced to disagree.

> ➢ When you are baptised into the body of Jesus, you are given a ministry, gifts and office (although you need to be *adopted* before you can begin operating in it). The point is; you are not given a "piece" of your ministry, but all of it.

1 Corinthians 12:13-20. *13 For by one Spirit are we all baptised into one body, whether we be Jews or Gentiles, whether we be bond or free; and have been all made to drink into one Spirit. 14 For the body is not one member, but many. 15 If the foot shall say, Because I am not the hand, I am not of the body; is it therefore not of the body? 16 And if the ear shall say, Because I am not the eye, I am not of the body; is it therefore not of the body? 17 If the whole body were an eye, where were the hearing? If the whole were hearing, where were the smelling? 18 But now hath God set the members every one of them in the body, as it has pleased him. 19 And if they were all one member, where were the body? 20 But now are they many members, yet one body.*

➢ When you are baptised with the Holy Spirit, you receive Him in all His fullness. There is no way you can be *partially filled*.
➢ When you enter the baptism of suffering, it is not just a part of you that suffers, but all of you.
➢ In the same way, water baptism must be complete in its symbol. If you die and are buried, they do not bury your head or forehead, but all of you.

Besides all this reasoning, let us look at the root word for 'baptism'.

It is a transliteration of the Greek word "baptizo" {according to Strong's lexicon [and its derivative words] (the numbers refer to the Strong's Concordance list): -

Greek 907 'baptizo'. . . .to make whelmed (i.e. fully wet); used only of ceremonial washing, especially. . .of the ordinance of Christian baptism: - baptist, baptize, wash.

Greek 908 Baptismata. . .baptism (technically and figuratively): - baptism.

Greek 909 Baptismos. . .ablution (ceremonial or Christian): - baptism, washing.

Greek 910 Baptistes. . .a baptizer,. . .Christ's forerunner: - Baptist.}

The meaning then, is to sink, submerge, dip, thoroughly wet, etc. Drawing a cross [or other thing] upon a person with water or sprinkling water or pouring water onto one's head does not constitute 'baptism'.

The only argument that people can raise from Scripture for these other forms of so – called *baptism* (as well as infant baptism); is based upon speculation. (e.g. Acts 16:33. These people speculate that there <u>must</u> have been babies in the house because the Word says *"all his 'house' was baptized"*.

Let us agree for *argument's sake*.

These babies <u>must</u> therefore have been intellectual giants; for the Word also states, in the same place, that *"they believed first, and all his house"* – Acts 16:31, 34. As I said: "pure speculation!" <u>If we do not follow the Word of God, our belief is in vain!</u>)

They [the misappropriators of the basic doctrines of Christ] also confuse circumcision, christening, child dedication, and baptism. Colossians 2:11 - 13. They link the dedication of an infant to God, with baptism.

In symbolism, we find the Israelites [the Believers] coming out of Egypt [the world and the satan's domain] and entering the Promised Land [the ministry the Believer is called to in all its power]. But, they have to cross the Red Sea [water baptism], the Jordan [Holy Spirit baptism] and enter and occupy the Promised

Land – with its giants [daily growing experiences] and its enemies [temptations, etc.]. Read Exodus 14.

Who Baptizes in Water?

This question is disputed by many Pastors, and scholars at seminary [Bible School]. The Word says that Believers do the baptizing. Nothing more, nothing less.

Matthew 28:18-20. *18 And Jesus came and spoke to them, saying, All power is given to me in heaven and earth. 19 You go therefore, and teach all nations, baptizing them in the name of the Father, and of the Son, and of the Holy Ghost: 20 Teaching them to observe all things whatsoever I have commanded you: and, know, I am with you always, [even] to the end of the world. Amen.*

It does not mention that it should be before witnesses. (Although, I believe it should be before witnesses as a witness to the world and as a standard for Christian commitment. Hebrews 12:1 tells us that a "great cloud of witnesses" surrounds us.

(1 Wherefore seeing we also are compassed about with so great a cloud of witnesses, let us lay aside every weight, and the sin which does so easily beset us, and let us run with patience the race that is set before us,)

[The devil and his minions, yes, but more importantly and significantly; we have the Triune God, the angels of God, all the Saints of God that have ever lived, as witnesses too.])

1 Timothy 6:12. *12 Fight the good fight of faith, lay hold on eternal life, whereunto you are also called, and have professed a good profession before many witnesses.*

Those that try to restrict the privilege of conducting baptism to their own domain, are of the insecure, ignorant and/or egotistical, disposition; or they are trying to build their own kingdom [as opposed to the kingdom of God]. Seldom is it for preservation of the Word, or Congregation sanctity, that they would object to allowing all Believers to practice it (although it could happen).

John the Baptist was the prophet of baptism Matthew 3:11. Jesus baptized His followers (although He himself did not baptize) John 4:1, 2. Jesus gives us all (Believers) instructions to baptize Matthew 28:19. See also John 14:15; Romans 6:4.

What is the significance of Water Baptism?

John the Baptist referred to his baptism as a "baptism unto repentance". The baptism in the Name of the Lord is the same but has the following added inference: -

➤ It includes a *cutting off* of the flesh, the circumcision of the heart – including the putting off of the *old man*
➤ Symbolising new beginnings [a new life] the old has passed away
➤ You are now identified, not only with the death, burial, and resurrection of Jesus, but with the Lord Jesus Christ Himself

➤ It includes the death of the self [will]. You choose to put the will of God first
➤ You are given a new name, the Name of the Lord Jesus Christ – you are now *in HIM*
➤ You experience a cleansing and renewal, although it is not the water that is doing the cleansing and renewing
➤ It cuts off the enemy's access to us forever
➤ You experience victory over sin in your life
➤ It requires true repentance on our part

We are baptized before a host of seen and unseen witnesses. We are declaring in three realms[50] that the symbolism portrayed in the flesh; is what has happened in reality, in the spirit. i.e. "I have died with Jesus, was buried with Jesus, and now, I have arisen with Jesus to die no more; and to live a separated life to God my Saviour."

Do you have a Responsibility after being Baptized?

Yes! You have to make a decision to practice what you have declared to the universe, in baptism.

• Say "Good Bye" to your old lifestyle. Cut ties with *bad* influences, and the ungodly lifestyles that go with it.
• Live within the new standard that the Lord has set for you.
• Be a disciple of Jesus. Learn from Him and about Him.
• Renew your mind to thinking that this is a <u>permanent</u> and special time of your life.

Who gets Baptized?

Only born-again children of God should be baptized. Acts 8:36 - 38; Luke 7:29, 30. This means that you cannot **become** *born-again* by baptism. You must be *born-again* before being baptized. You cannot join a Congregation or become a Christian through baptism.

Baptised in Whose Name?

There is much ado about the name in which you get baptized. So, let us, at this point consider a few relevant Names of God. God identifies Himself and expects us to accept what he says about Himself. He does not reveal Himself in one 'fell-swoop'. The Lord knows that we would not be able to handle the revelation of all His Names all at once. So He wisely introduces Himself *one Name at a time*. These names, as one would understand if they were Jewish, indicate His nature and character. God reveals Himself as:

- LORD (Jehovah) – Exodus 3:14, 15; 15:3; Isaiah 42:8, etc.
- I AM – Exodus 3:14, 15; John 8:58.
- Jesus – Luke 1:31; Matthew 1:21.
- Christ – John 1:41; Acts 10:38.

God named Jesus. God identifies Himself as the 'LORD'. Jesus identifies Himself with/as God the Father. The Holy Spirit is referred to as the anointing that confirms that Jesus of Nazareth is the 'Christ'. As we use the name "Lord Jesus Christ", we are using the Name of the triune God, in His fullness. Another name that does the same is 'Elohim'.

Being baptized in the Name of the <u>Lord Jesus Christ</u> is the same, therefore, as being baptized in the Name of Jesus, the Name of the Lord (Jehovah), or even the Name of Christ! Please, let us lay to rest the foolish debate as to the Name in which to be baptised. As long as you are involved in Christian baptism, being baptized in either of these names is acceptable with the LORD.

Another unscriptural practice is the one where the *Baptizer* "dunks" the *Baptizee* (the one being baptized) once for each of the "members" of the Godhead. . ."I baptize you on the name of the Father. . ." – DUNK, ". . .and of the Son. . ." – DUNK, ". . .and of the Holy Spirit." – DUNK. No! It is "I baptize you in the Name of the Father, and of the Son, and of the Holy Spirit." – Dunk. There is NO Scriptural reason or precedence for the three-times-dunk.

When do you get Baptized?

After you believe; Acts 8:12 (*But when they believed Philip preaching the things concerning the kingdom of God, and the name of Jesus Christ, they were baptized, both men and women.*); Acts 2:38 (*Then Peter said unto them, Repent, and be baptized every one of you in the name of Jesus Christ for the remission of sins, and you shall receive the gift of the Holy Ghost.*).

Here we see God's pattern for the Christian life and for baptism.

- **The first step is death**; Romans 6:4 [*Therefore we are buried with him by baptism into death: that like as Christ was raised up from the dead by the glory of the*

Father, even so we also should walk in newness of life.]
(**This is the *repent* part**).
- **The second step is burial;** Colossians 2:12
  [*Buried with him in baptism, wherein also you are risen with him through the faith of the operation of God, who has raised him from the dead.*](**This is [all] the *baptisms* part**).
- **The third step is resurrection;** 1 Corinthians
  15:3, 4 [3 *For I delivered unto you first of all that which I also received, how that Christ died for our sins according to the scriptures; 4 And that he was buried, and that he rose again the third day according to the scriptures:*]
  (**This is the *believe/receive* part**).

One Baptism?

(Note on Mark 16:16 and Ephesians 4:4-6.)
When we take the Word of God as our authority and there seems to be a conflict or a contradiction, then we need to look further than just a normal reading of the word/s in the Bible. Water Baptism cannot save you, and this is clear from Scriptures like Ephesians 2:8, 9. (8 *For by grace are you saved through faith; and that not of yourselves: it is the gift of God: 9 Not of works, lest any man should boast.*) Still, some folk will point out that there is **one baptism** and by *that* baptism one is **saved** as in Ephesians 4:5. So let us look at this for a moment.

Ephesians 4:4-6. 4 *There is one body, and one Spirit, even as you are called in one hope of your calling; 5 One Lord, one faith, one baptism, 6 One God and Father of all, who is above all, and through all, and in you all.*

150

Mark 16:16. *16 He that believes and is baptized shall be saved; but he that believes not shall be damned.*

As I have said previously, the word 'baptism' has a plural implication. (Hebrews 6:1, 2, Ephesians 4:5 and Mark 16:16.) The word is used in Scripture in both singular and plural applications. [e.g. Mark 10:38, John 1:33; 3:26; Romans 6:4; Acts 1:5 {both}; 2:38, 41; 19:4; 1 Peter 3:21.] Ephesians 4:5 can then accurately be rendered the result of **one baptisms**.

Taking this a step further, allow me to quote Dr. Zodhiates, from his "Hebrew-Greek Key Study Bible's Lexical aids to the New Testament" for the word 'baptize'.

"907. Baptizo;. . . in its general signification means to identify with. . . baptism in. . . Holy Ghost. . . into the Body of Christ. . . grievous afflictions and sufferings." (Examples and Scriptures are given in his text.)

And. . .

"908. Baptisma;. . . The suffix 'ma' indicates the result of the act of dipping. . ." (As in Ephesians 4:5.)

Let me now quote Dr. Zodhiates, from his "Hebrew-Greek Key Study Bible's Lexical aids to the New Testament" for the word "Saved".

4982. Sozo; to save,. . .

1) . . . temporal deliverance from danger, suffering,. . .
2) . . .the spiritual and eternal salvation. . . by those who believe on Christ. . . from bondage of sin. . .
4) . . .the future. . . at the second coming. . . saving."

(Examples and Scriptures are given in his text.)

Both the words for *saved* and *baptism* must be looked at correctly/simultaneously. *Saved* is not only *born-again*. It embraces the whole spectrum of the Christian lifestyle! That is a past, present, and future application. *Baptism*, as you can now see is inclusive of <u>all</u> the forms of baptism mentioned in the Bible and should never be separated, except for study and when they are practised (the ideal would be to be born-again, water baptized and filled with the Holy Spirit at 'one sitting' so that the person would be fully prepared for the baptism of suffering they are about to embark upon; but that is not always possible).

So then, if a person *believes* [is born-again], and is *baptized* [in obedience], where is the misunderstanding? He will be *saved*. The only thing we need to avoid is reading into the sentence that baptism is necessary for salvation.

Chapter End Notes

47 Literally, "in the heavenlies". The same Greek word is used in John 3:12, where "things" is added (which is unfortunate). In both places the word signifies that which is heavenly in contradistinction to that which is earthly. In Ephesians "places" (as found in the King James Version and other similar versions) is especially misleading. "The heavenlies" may be defined as the sphere of the Believer's spiritual experience as identified with Christ in nature (2 Peter 1:4); life (Colossians 3:4); service (Matthew 28:20; John 17:18); suffering (Philippians 1:29; 3:10; Colossians 1:24); inheritance (Romans 8:16,17); and future glory in the kingdom (Romans 8:18-21; 1 Peter 2:9; Revelations 1:6; 5:10). The Believer is a heavenly man, and a stranger and pilgrim on the earth (Hebrews 3:1; 1 Peter 2:11).

48 "Adoption" (Greek 'huiothesia' meaning 'place as a son') is not so much a word of relationship as of position. A Jewish child would be cared for by his mother and the Torah is taught to him until he is twelve years old (mostly memorizing the Torah) [*Luke 2:42, 46. 42 And when he was twelve years old, they went up to Jerusalem after the custom of the feast 46 And it came to pass, that after three days they found him in the temple, sitting in the midst of the doctors, both hearing them, and asking them questions.*]. If the child impressed the "Doctors" – Teachers – Rabbis – of the 'Law' – Tanakh, they would be selected to be invited to be taught by that 'Doctor', at his "Bar Mitzvah" (the party to celebrate their reaching the age of Manhood). They would enter the "Rabbinical School", which lasted until they were 30 years old. If they were obviously anointed by the Lord (there

were certain criteria for this, of which I shall not go into here) then they would be recognized by the Rabbinical "order", and hands would be laid upon them and the "authority" transferred to them. They would then have the authority to choose "Disciples" for themselves and teach those disciples.

Should the child fail to enter a Rabbi's School, then they would have their "Bar Mitzvah" (the party to celebrate their age of Manhood) and their father would train them in his trade. Should he pick it up well and be able to take it over from his father, his father would 'Adopt' him. This means that his father's business would become his; and he would have the honour of allowing his father to work for him until he retired; and ultimately care for him in his old age.

49 Reading Galatians 3:29 to Galatians 4:3, puts this Scripture into a glorious perspective. It does refer to Jesus as the Heir and Lord of all, but it also refers to us as God's children, who are also heirs and co-heirs with Christ (Romans 8:17). Bringing home a wonderful revelation that has been lost to the Church for centuries. (i.e. That we are able to claim our inheritance, in this life, of such great magnitude that it boggles the mind that lacks faith.)

50 The realms of the 'natural' or physical, the realm of Heaven, and the realm of the devil or hell.

Chapter 10

Baptism into the Holy Ghost

Holy Spirit or Holy Ghost?

The Holy Spirit, or Holy Ghost, is the same important *third* Person of the Trinity. Some people are au fait (conversant) with the term and meaning of "Ghost", while others are more familiar with the term and meaning of "Spirit". They mean and imply the same thing (although 'Ghost' may have a more 'negative' connotation). One name is not more 'holy' than the other. While others, again [particularly due to language differences], may picture "Ghost" as an evil spectre and find it offensive {I think particularly of the Chinese or Afrikaans languages}. Maybe, here, there is a call for being sensitive to other's preferences.

Who is the Holy Spirit?

The Holy Spirit, or Holy Ghost, is the third person of the Trinity (Father, Son [Jesus], and Holy Spirit). He is <u>not</u> a *thing*, as some would understand Him. He is not the least of the Holy Trinity just because He is mentioned last. He **is** the power of the Trinity. He is the *silent* worker and helper of the Children of God. He is called the following, in the Bible: -

> ➤ The Helper ("Paraclete" – 'one who comes alongside to help') - John 14:26
> ➤ The Spirit of Truth – John 14:16,17
> ➤ The Spirit of Jesus – Galatians 4:6

It is He that gives us the strength and ability to be witnesses for Jesus. It is He that gives us the ability to perform miracles, healing, etc., and it is He that empowers us to practice the gifts.

General Comments

Baptism in the Holy Spirit is when you ask Jesus to baptize you in the Holy Spirit. The Holy Spirit then gives you power to become witnesses and martyrs for God. {Notice please, the work is done <u>by</u> Jesus, that is: – filling you with *power to perform*.}

The promise of this baptism, that God gave man, can be summed up like this: -

Man reigning with God within. (Adam reigned with God without. Now, God can come into us in His fullness.) More importantly, it is God's sign to us that He has seen and accepted our commitment to him! (See 'baptism' in the 'I.V.P. Bible dictionary vol. 1.')

The work of the Holy Spirit was and is healing; convicting; drawing to God; giving peace/power/ etc.; guiding; prophesying; and so on. We also find the Holy Spirit coming upon people in the Old Testament. The difference is that in the Old Testament the Holy Spirit was given on a conditional basis. It depended on your response and your obedience. If you failed, you lost the Holy Spirit.

In the *New Testament* the Holy Spirit is unconditional and He now can live within you. Another difference is that you speak in an unlearned language. This is the *evidence* that the Holy Spirit is in you. Speaking in tongues, builds your faith, personally. This experience is only possible through the application of the blood of Jesus.

When you become a Believer, you receive an *earnest* or deposit of the Holy Spirit in the form of the *Spirit of Jesus* (Galatians 4:6). The Holy Spirit, being the deposit at salvation, may raise another question. <u>Must</u> you have more of the Holy Spirit? Or do you have all that is available?

It is a requirement of God that you receive the <u>fullness</u> of the Holy Spirit. It is a principle that you finish what you started. It is foolish to take a bit when you have a lot available to you. Let's look at the 'ten virgins. . .' Matthew 25:1-12.

Matthew 25:1 – 12. *1 Then shall the kingdom of heaven be likened unto ten virgins, which took their lamps, and went forth to meet the bridegroom. 2 And five of them were wise, and five were foolish. 3 They that were foolish took their lamps, and took no oil with them: 4 But the wise took oil in their vessels with their lamps. 5 While the bridegroom tarried, they all slumbered and slept. 6 And at midnight there was a cry made, Behold, the bridegroom comes; you go out to meet him. 7 Then all those virgins arose, and trimmed their lamps. 8 And the foolish said unto the wise, Give us of your oil; for our lamps are gone out. 9 But the wise answered, saying, Not so; lest there be not enough for us and you: but you go rather to them that sell, and buy for yourselves. 10 And while they went to buy, the bridegroom came; and they that were ready went in with him to the marriage: and the door was shut. 11 Afterward came also the other virgins, saying, Lord, Lord, open to us. 12 But he answered and said, Verily I say unto you, I know you not.*

This is a separate experience after being *born-again*. It is called being *filled* or *baptized* with the Holy Spirit. The disciples were instructed by Jesus to wait until they received the promised power. This happened when the Holy Spirit came upon them and they began to speak with *tongues* (or the unlearned language). These people were already born-again and disciples of Jesus. In fact, some of them were apostles.

John 20:22, 23. *22 And when he had said this, he breathed on [them], and said to them, Receive the Holy Ghost: 23 Whosoever sins you remit, they are remitted to them; [and] whosoever [sins] you retain, they are retained.*

Acts 1:8 shows us that they only became witnesses after they received the baptism of the Holy Spirit.

(But you shall receive power, after that the Holy Ghost is come upon you: and you shall be witnesses unto me both in Jerusalem, and in all Judaea, and in Samaria, and unto the uttermost part of the earth.)

(See the excellent book on the Holy Spirit called "The Spirit Himself" by Ralph M. Riggs.)

Baptism in the Holy Spirit Promised

God has promised us the Holy Spirit, with the
evidence of speaking in tongues, in the Old Testament.
And, God keeps His promises!

> Isaiah 28:11, 12. *11 For with stammering lips and
> another tongue will he speak to this people. 12 To
> whom he said, This is the rest wherewith you may
> cause the weary to rest; and this is the refreshing: yet
> they would not hear.*

The '*stammering lips and another tongue*' sounds sus-
piciously like the speaking in our heavenly language.
As one speaks in tongues, there is an effect of a rest
that floods your spirit, and indeed, it is refreshing!

> Joel 2:28, 29. *28 And it shall come to pass afterward,
> that I will pour out my spirit upon all flesh; and your
> sons and your daughters shall prophesy, your old
> men shall dream dreams, your young men shall see
> visions: 29 And also upon the servants and upon the
> handmaidens in those days will I pour out my spirit.*

To illustrate the idea that the Spirit of God would
come upon everyone that wanted Him, Joel mentions
sons, daughters, old and young men. This is easily
understood, but then he mentions men and women
servants separately.

Why would this be?

In those days, servants were treated with less concern than an animal, say, a dog. When the dog came up
to its owner, it would be petted. But a servant doing his
job would not receive even a "thank you" because it
was his duty and it was expected of him to have done

the task given to him. Even upon these servants, God would pour out His Spirit. What a promise. . .there is hope for every one of us!

Jesus does the Baptizing

A man cannot baptize any other man in the Holy Spirit. Only Jesus can do that; only Jesus has *access* to the Holy Spirit with which to baptize.

Matthew 3:11. *11 I indeed baptize you with water unto repentance: but he that comes after me is mightier than I, whose shoes I am not worthy to bear: he shall baptize you with the Holy Ghost, and with fire:*

Mark 1:8. *8 I indeed have baptized you with water: but he shall baptize you with the Holy Ghost.*

The Promise Fulfilled

Here you see the integrity of God once again. . .He pours out the Holy Spirit as He promised!

Acts 1:4, 8. *8 And, being assembled together with them, commanded them that they should not depart from Jerusalem, but wait for the promise of the Father, which, says he, you have heard of me. 8 But you shall receive power after the Holy Ghost is come upon you: and you shall be witnesses unto me both in Jerusalem, and in all Judaea, and in Samaria, and unto the uttermost part of the earth.*

Not only are we now able to receive the Holy Spirit baptism, but we (the Gentiles) are now able to be grafted into the 'Olive Tree'; all since the day that the Holy Spirit was poured out on the disciples[51]. In the same way, you are included in the Congregation (world-wide) when you are baptized in the Holy Spirit!

Conversely, if you are not baptized in the Holy Spirit, you are not part of the True Congregation. This is perhaps a controversial thought and could do with an explanation. So I refer you to my end note on the topic[52].

<u>Tongues – the Evidence</u>

When you get baptized in water, you do not clench your fists, squeeze your eyes shut and mutter under your breath "Please let me be wet. . .Please let me be wet. . .Please let me be wet. . ." It is part and parcel of being baptized in water. . .you get wet! In the same way, as you concentrate upon being filled with the Almighty Holy Spirit, you shall become so saturated that you will not be able to stop yourself speaking in tongues. . .(well, if you refuse to speak, then you <u>could</u>, possibly; I would have to ask why then would you ask to be baptized in the Holy Spirit, if you did not want to speak in the Holy Spirit's language, in the first place?).

Acts 2:4. 4 And they were all filled with the Holy Ghost, and began to speak with other tongues, as the Spirit gave them utterance.

Acts 10:44-46. 44 While Peter yet spoke these words, the Holy Ghost fell on all them which heard the word. 45 And they of the circumcision which believed were astonished, as many as came with Peter, because that on the Gentiles also was poured out the gift of the Holy Ghost. 46 For they heard them speak with tongues, and magnify God. Then answered Peter,

Tongues – Unintelligible Secrets

1 Corinthians 14:2. 2 For he that speaks in an unknown tongue speaks not unto men, but unto God: for no man understands him; howbeit in the spirit he speaks mysteries.

A meaning in the Hebrew text indicates that the *mysteries* here refer to the destiny of the speaker. He that speaks in tongues is speaking out his destiny in the Lord. (Dr. Zodhiates Hebrew-Greek Key Study Bible.)

There is a difference between speaking in private and speaking in public. Many people get the two confused and expect public speaking in private and private speaking in public. When it does not work out, they try to accuse the principle and Spirit of being *false.*

There are many experiences that folk have had in speaking in tongues. We normally refer to them as our *heavenly tongue.* But often, it is actually more accurate to say *an unlearned language.*

I have personally heard a South African lady speaking in a Chinese dialect. A story I heard was of a Jew being present when someone spoke aloud in his spiritual language. The Jew later spoke to him to ask where he had learned Hebrew. It was then discovered that he had spoken a pure Hebrew message that convicted that Jew to serve the Lord Jesus. And the man had never even heard Hebrew spoken before, let alone having learned to speak it.

God Speaking through Man in Tongues

As Jesus is a *Life-giving Spirit* and enters your spirit to give you New Birth, so the Holy Spirit enters your spirit to give it power. Part of that power is the power of speech. In effect, the Holy Spirit speaks through your spirit.

1 Corinthians 14:21. *21 In the law it is written, With men of other tongues and other lips will I speak unto this people; and yet for all that will they not hear me, says the Lord.*

See here that the Scripture says '. . .will I speak. . .' and '. . .says the Lord.'

The Spirit is Subject to the Prophet

You can choose when and where to speak in the Spirit. In this way you *control* the Spirit within you.

1 Corinthians 14:32. *32 And the spirits of the prophets are subject to the prophets.*

If you are born-again and filled with the Holy Spirit, God calls you a *Prophet*. The Holy Spirit will not burst out of you speaking without Him allowing you to do the speaking. So, you will not be in a supermarket (as an example) and suddenly become vocal in an unknown tongue. You must always choose to speak.

Who will Speak in Tongues?

Mark 16:17. *17 And these signs shall follow them that believe; In my name shall they cast out devils; they shall speak with new tongues;*

If you believe and receive, you will be speaking in tongues. You find two types of speaking in tongues. One is your personal, private time of prayer that builds your faith – Jude 20. The other is speaking in tongues in public meetings – prayer meetings, Congregation meetings, etc. - 1 Corinthians chapters 12 and 14.

Reason for Personal Tongues[53]

Jude 20. *20 But you, beloved, building up yourselves on your most holy faith, praying in the Holy Ghost,*

Prayer to Receive the Holy Spirit

"Jesus, baptize me in the Holy Spirit, and I will speak in tongues as the Holy Spirit gives me the words." This is the simplest and most Scriptural prayer one can pray to receive the Holy Spirit baptism. Any added words will be so much "hot air". Extra words may seem to sound "holy" but they are totally superfluous.

Advice on Receiving the Holy Spirit Baptism

Forget about *speaking in tongues*. Start to look for the Holy Spirit to just come and soak you through with Himself. As you concentrate on the *giver* of the tongues, you shall receive the tongues as well. As with the woman with the issue of blood, determine to receive from Jesus. Seek a *point of contact*[54]. Use your

God given imagination. (This practice should also be used for receiving your healing, anointing, presence of God, entering into heaven in worship, etc.) You are the temple of the Holy Spirit and need to be filled.

Try to imagine yourself as a vessel. Imagine Jesus standing above and before you with an earthen jug in His hands. As you pray the above prayer, imagine Jesus pouring out the water from the jug; and it becomes a river flowing just above your head. (Water is one of the symbols of the Holy Spirit.)

Press your face into the stream and drink this water in. Imagine how it begins to fill you from your feet up. When your whole body is saturated, you are ready to simply begin speaking the words, which will be your own *heavenly language*.

Some folk imagine themselves being filled with the Holy Spirit quicker than others. Therefore do not allow yourself to be pressurized, God is in no hurry and will not fail you. If YOU choose not to speak out in this language, you will be disappointing no one but yourself. So, reject timidity, inferiority, self-consciousness, embarrassment, etc. Remember also, the Lord will not move your mouth. That is your 'job'.

Your mouth may become dry, like it is full of cotton wool. You may feel nervous. You may feel you have clammy palms, and so on. This is normal! Remember, you have asked the Power of the God, who spoke worlds into existence, to come and live in your heart. It is a *supernatural* experience and one that is awesome beyond words. Hey! We are human, you know! Do not worry, you will not offend the Lord and He will not rush you.

Some Scriptures

➤ <u>Holy Spirit Work</u> Genesis 1:2; Genesis 6:3; Genesis 41:38.
<u>Earnest</u> 2 Corinthians 1:22; 2 Corinthians 5:5; Ephesians 1:14; Ephesians 4:30.
➤ <u>10 virgins</u> Matthew 25:1 - 13.
<u>Holy Spirit is the Promise</u> Matthew 3:11; Matthew 12:31, 32; John 1:33; John 20:22; Acts 2:4 (see footnote below); Acts 2:33, 38; Acts 7:51; Acts 8:15, 17; Acts 10:38; Romans 15:13; 1 Thessalonians 1:5; 1 Thessalonians 4:8.
➤ <u>Commitment Principle</u> Luke 14:27 - 35.

Important Footnotes

Genesis 9:16. *16 And the bow shall be in the cloud; and I will look upon it, that I may remember the everlasting covenant[55] between every living creature of all flesh that is upon the earth.*

God is a keeper of covenants! He is FAITHFUL and cannot have His Word *broken*. This applies to ANY covenant He makes.

Acts 2:4. *4 And they were all filled with the Holy[56] Ghost, and began to speak with other tongues, as the Spirit gave them utterance.*

The footnote on *Holy Ghost* in Acts 2:4, explains more thoughts than I do, in the course of this study.

Rabbit Trail Starts. . .

The Perfect Opportunity to Define the Antichrist

As you study the Word of God, you shall come across a character called the *antichrist*. Besides the Godhead, this character is referred to most in the Bible. As the name implies and is readily understandable, he is the one that stands against Christ. Taking into account that Jesus is the "Anointed One, and His anointing", which is a definition for "Christ" simplified and made popular by Dr. Creflo Dollar, you can understand that the antichrist will be against Jesus, the Christ. He will also be against the Holy Spirit because it is the Holy Spirit that anoints, not just Jesus, but us as well. In short, the antichrist shall oppose, resist, belittle and otherwise despise anything to do with the Holy Spirit (mainly), as well as despise Jesus our Lord.

((1 John 2:18) Little children, it is the last time: and as you have heard that antichrist shall come, even now are there many antichrists; whereby we know that it is the last time.

(1 John 2:22) Who is a liar but he that denies that Jesus is the Christ? He is antichrist, that denies the Father and the Son.

(1 John 4:3) And every spirit that confesses not that Jesus Christ is come in the flesh is not of God: and this is that spirit of antichrist, whereof you have heard that it should come; and even now already is it in the world.

167

(2 John 1:7) For many deceivers are entered into the world, who confess not that Jesus Christ is come in the flesh. This is a deceiver and an antichrist.)

This is, unfortunately, not the only deception and attack that shall be levelled at our Lord and Saviour and the precious Holy Spirit, our Teacher, Guide and Friend. The most deceptive is going to be that he shall attempt to usurp the station /position of the true Christ. In other words he shall perform miracles, speak peace, and sound so religious that some may be fooled into thinking that he is Jesus, the Christ. He shall claim to have come back to earth or at the very least, appear as the awaited 'Christ' (whatever their concept of *christ* may be). He may call himself something else (besides *Jesus Christ*) but he shall attempt to claim worldly power and authority from God. He shall try and portray Jesus, our Lord (the <u>real</u> Jesus Christ), as the villain. It seems that he will be VERY convincing. Fortunately, the true Holy Spirit has revealed his strategy and warned us ahead of time.

There has been a spate of people claiming to be the *Christ* (as examples: - John Denver, Bob Marley, David Koresh, to name a few of the more well-known ones). He shall claim that you can easily call him "Mahadi", "the Fifth Buddha", or a variety of other mystical names as well as 'normal' names. The bottom line is that the definition of antichrist is not just to "resist" or "oppose" but also to "imitate" or "replace" the true Christ. He shall be anti-Trinity, anti-Son, anti-Crucifixion, and anti-God-in-the-flesh (among other things).

(1 John 4:1-3. 1 Beloved, believe not every spirit, but try the spirits whether they are of God: because many false prophets are gone out into the world. 2

Hereby you know the Spirit of God: Every spirit that confesses that Jesus Christ is come in the flesh is of God: 3 And every spirit that confesses not that Jesus Christ is come in the flesh is not of God: and this is that spirit of antichrist, whereof you have heard that it should come; and even now already is it in the world.)

He shall also start his 'career' in a peaceful and friendly way, but it will only take a few years before his true colours show through. He shall demand obeisance (worship), obedience and total control of the world and even individual lives; but, he shall not control the whole world.

A parting thought. For there to be an *antichrist*, there has to first be a true Christ! No one has ever made a counterfeit R3-00 (Rand) note (or dollar or pound or whatever currency you have) in the history of the Rand. Why would that be? There is no such thing as a R3-00 note! The same would apply with those claiming to be agnostics, atheists, etc. You cannot disbelieve something unless there is a *something* to disbelieve.

Rabbit Trail Ends. . .

Baptism in suffering

John 15:1-8. 1 I am the true vine and my Father is the husbandman. 2 Every branch in me that bears no fruit he takes away: and every [branch] that bears fruit, he purges it, that it may bring forth more fruit. 3 Now you are clean through the word that I have spoken to you. 4 Abide in me, and I in you. As the branch cannot bear fruit of itself, except it abide in the vine; no more can you, except you abide in me. 5

I am the vine, you [are] the branches: he that abides in me, and I in him, the same brings forth much fruit: for without me you can do nothing. 6 If a man abide not in me, he is cast forth as a branch, and is withered; and men gather them, and cast [them] into the fire, and they are burned. 7 If you abide in me, and my words abide in you, you shall ask what you will, and it shall be done to you. 8 Herein is my Father glorified, that you bear much fruit; so shall you be my disciples.

Galatians 5:22 speaks of *fruit* of the Spirit, not *fruits*. It is one fruit but has nine parts to it, like a bunch of grapes. It is one fruit – a bunch of grapes – but has nine *units* – individual grapes. The fruit of the Spirit is one fruit with nine *evidences* – Love[57], Joy[58], Peace[59], Longsuffering[60], Gentleness[61], Goodness[62], Faith[63], Meekness[64] and Temperance[65].

The Baptism of Suffering could be likened to trimming branches in your life, which are always by means of painful events. These painful events may take the form of: -

➤ Experiences
➤ Circumstances
➤ Unfair treatment
➤ Supernatural   pressure/events/experiences/ call it what you will

Always. . .it is God's hand working in your life and forming character and. . .
Never. . .is it in the form of a penal action against you.
Suffering <u>shall</u> come! Just because you are *in Christ*, and often, for no other reason. Every believer will suffer or they will never reign with Jesus. {Notice please, the

170

work is done <u>by</u> the Holy Spirit that is: – cutting the old nature from you.}

It is not God's will for you to suffer [in vain]; He uses it to make you more like Christ Jesus. You suffer <u>as</u> Jesus did <u>because</u> Jesus suffered. The reason for our suffering is found in that man has rejected God, and they will reject you [because of your association with Him]. If you are willing to suffer because of your righteousness (natural man hates righteousness because it convicts him of his own sin), you will receive a reward. Suffering for Christ qualifies you for this reward. *Baptism in suffering* means that suffering becomes part of your life.

<u>This suffering does not include sickness</u>. God might allow sickness by using it (if you already have it), but it has <u>never</u> been God's designed tool in the experience of suffering.

Do not misunderstand, if you are an unfruitful branch, God will remove you from the earth. God's purpose for you is to bring forth *lasting (eternal)* fruit. If you are not *pruned*, you will be over-burdened and you shall break (as a natural tree would). This is a part of God's wisdom and love for you. . .to suffer righteously.

You must keep a right attitude towards the baptism of suffering. You can reject the baptism of suffering; in the same way you can reject all the other baptisms.

- You do not have to become a Christian. But, you will go to hell.
- You do not have to be baptised in water. But, you will be in disobedience.
- You do not have to receive the Holy Spirit. But, you will be rejecting God and His supernatural power.
- You do not have to accept suffering – but then you will not have the character of Christ formed in you. Nor will you reign, nor will you mature, nor will you receive that reward.

Having the right attitude pleases God. Receiving the baptisms with a wrong attitude makes you a hypocrite. The attitude in suffering is not with your eye on the reward. Jesus suffered for you, returning the honour will make you one with Jesus. The more you become like Jesus, the more reward you receive – with more suffering.

The reward would be *automatic*. Like: -

o   Repentance receives Forgiveness.
o   Baptism in water makes you wet
o   Baptism in the Holy Spirit causes you to speak in Tongues

The point is: do not focus upon what you can obtain *from the Lord* – be grateful – sure, but do not "obsess" about it.

What is suffering in God's eyes? Very simple! Giving up what is morally, ethically, possessionally, and rightfully, yours.

If you give up some food for Jesus, you are suffering. If you lose face or honour for Jesus, you are suffering. If you suffer loss of anything, any person (friend or foe), for the sake of the Gospel, you are suffering for Christ. This could include physical suffering as the Martyrs did in the past; and as persecution that certain countries are experiencing, even today.

There may come a time in your life, and I could say there **shall** come a time in your life, where you will have to make a public stand for Jesus at the peril of losing something you value. It could be your honour, your pride, your possessions, your family, your friends, or your life. Set it in your mind that it will come, and it is not because of anything you have done wrong – although they will make it sound like that is the case.

Read Philippians 2:3 – 10 but especially verses 5 and 8. (*5 Let this mind be in you, which was also in Christ Jesus: 8 And being found in fashion as a man, he humbled himself, and became obedient unto death, even the death of the cross.*)

When reading the accounts of Saints dying, God does not seem at all perturbed about their deaths, in fact the Word says that God *delights* in the death of His Saints (Psalms 116:15 *Precious in the sight of the LORD is the death of his saints.*). This is not because He is morbid or sadistic. God knows that the Spiritual is more real than the physical, and, His Saint is coming home to Him! He loves you so much that it excites Him to have you come home to be with Him. It is us that fear death because we lose sight of the reality of God, Heaven and the Eternity promised to us.

Let us examine 2 Corinthians 1:5 - 7.

2 Corinthians 1:5 (*For as the sufferings of Christ abound in us, so our consolation also abounds by Christ.*)

If the suffering of Christ abounds **in** us, then the consolation abounds **by** Christ too.

2 Corinthians 1:6 (*And whether we be afflicted, it is for your consolation and salvation, which is effectual in the enduring of the same sufferings which we also suffer: or whether we be comforted, it is for your consolation and salvation.*)

If we are afflicted, then we receive consolation and salvation, (Consolation and Salvation are both effective in us while enduring the suffering) because the *Comforting* is the Consolation and Salvation. God does the consoling which brings us comfort in the fact that God's integrity guarantees our salvation; and this knowledge comforts us.

2 Corinthians 1:7 (*And our hope of you is stedfast, knowing, that as you are partakers of the sufferings, so shall you be also of the consolation.*)

Our hope is stedfast. We are partakers of the suffering; therefore we are partakers of the Consolation.

This all sounds like a lot of repetition. And maybe it is, but the importance of understanding this principle justifies the repetition. We need to be comforted, especially in a painful situation. Our experiences of suffering may qualify as *a painful situation.*

Let us now look at the individual words and see if we can increase our understanding of this passage (using the Strong's Lexicon).

174

- <u>Consolation</u> 3874 Paraklesis from - solace, imploration: - Comfort, exhortation, intreaty.
- <u>Comfort</u> 3870 Parafaleo from 3844 & 2564 to call near, i.e. invite, invoke: - Beseech, call for, (be of good) comfort, desire, (give) exhort (ation), intreat, pray.
- <u>Patience</u> 420 Anexikakos from 430 & 2556; enduring of ill, i.e. forbearing: - Patient.

A word that is strongly linked to suffering is *patience*. Sometimes, the word *patience* is used interchangeably with the word *suffering*. And, other times, it is used in place of it; but always, the words are used with the connotation of bearing ill against yourself without becoming bitter and holding a grudge.

Another thought, at the time of the suffering experience, the Lord is very near to you.

Allow the Scriptures to Speak

Matthew 5:11 - 12. *11 Blessed are you, when men shall revile you, and persecute you, and shall say all manner of evil against you falsely, for my sake. 12 Rejoice, and be exceeding glad: for great is your reward in heaven: for so persecuted they the prophets which were before you.* – Jesus teaches on suffering.

Matthew 16:21. *21 From that time forth began Jesus to shew unto his disciples, how that he must go unto Jerusalem, and suffer many things of the elders and chief priests and scribes, and be killed, and be raised again the third day.*

Matthew 17:12. *12 But I say unto you, That Elias is come already, and they knew him not, but have done unto him whatsoever they listed.(desired) Likewise shall also the Son of man suffer of them.*

Matthew 20:22. *22 But Jesus answered and said, Ye know not what you ask. Are you able to drink of the cup that I shall drink of, and to be baptized with the baptism that I am baptized with? They say unto him, We are able.*

Mark 8:31. *31 And he began to teach them, that the Son of man must suffer many things, and be rejected of the elders, and of the chief priests, and scribes, and be killed, and after three days rise again.*

Mark 10:38. *38 But Jesus said unto them, You know not what you ask: can you drink of the cup that I drink of? and be baptized with the baptism that I am baptized with?*

Luke 12:50. *50 But I have a baptism to be baptized with; and how am I straitened till it be accomplished!* – Baptism of suffering.

Luke 22:15. *15 And he said unto them, With desire I have desired to eat this passover with you before I suffer:* – Jesus suffered.

John 3:19 - 21. *19 And this is the condemnation, that light is come into the world, and men loved darkness rather than light, because their deeds were evil. 20 For every one that does evil hates the light, neither comes to the light, lest his deeds should be reproved. 21 But he that does truth comes to the light, that his deeds may be made manifest, that they are wrought in God.*

Acts 9:16. *16 For I will show him how great things he must suffer for my name's sake.* – Paul suffered.

Acts 26:23. *23 That Christ should suffer, and that he should be the first that should rise from the dead, and should show light unto the people, and to the Gentiles.* – Reigning and raising from the dead go hand-in-hand.

Romans 8:17. *17 And if children, then heirs; heirs of God, and joint-heirs with Christ; if so be that we suffer with him, that we may be also glorified together.*

1 Corinthians 4:12. *12 And labour, working with our own hands: being reviled, we bless; being persecuted, we suffer it:*

1 Corinthians 6:7. *7 Now therefore there is utterly a fault among you, because you go to law one with another. Why do you not rather take wrong? why do you not rather suffer yourselves to be defrauded?*

1 Corinthians 10:13. *13 There has no temptation taken you but such as is common to man: but God is faithful, who will not suffer you to be tempted above that you are able; but will with the temptation also make a way to escape, that you may be able to bear it.* – Take you through, not out.

1 Corinthians 12:26. *26 And whether one member suffer, all the members suffer with it; or one member be honoured, all the members rejoice with it.* – All suffer together.

2 Corinthians 1:6. *6 And whether we be afflicted, it is for your consolation and salvation, which is effectual in the enduring of the same sufferings which we also suffer: or whether we be comforted, it is for your consolation and salvation.* – Leaders suffer for their followers.

Galatians 5:11. *11 And I, brethren, if I yet preach circumcision, why do I yet suffer persecution? then is the offence of the cross ceased.*

Galatians 6:12. *12 As many as desire to make a fair show in the flesh, they constrain you to be circumcised; only lest they should suffer persecution for the cross of Christ.*

Philippians 1:29. *29 For unto you it is given in the behalf of Christ, not only to believe on him, but also to suffer for his sake;* – We are to suffer for Jesus.

1 Thessalonians 3:4. *4 For verily, when we were with you, we told you before that we should suffer tribulation; even as it came to pass, and you know.* – Suffering will come.

2 Thessalonians 1:5, *5 Which is a manifest token of the righteous judgment of God, that you may be counted worthy of the kingdom of God, for which you also suffer: –* <u>You counted worthy to suffer</u>.

1 Timothy 4:10. *10 For therefore we both labour and suffer reproach, because we trust in the living God, who is the Saviour of all men, specially of those that believe.*

2 Timothy 1:12. *12 For the which cause I also suffer these things: nevertheless I am not ashamed: for I know whom I have believed, and am persuaded that he is able to keep that which I have committed unto him against that day.*

2 Timothy 2:9. *9 Wherein I suffer trouble, as an evil doer, even unto bonds; but the word of God is not bound. –* <u>These are examples of suffering</u>.

2 Timothy 2:12. *12 If we suffer, we shall also reign with him: if we deny him, he also will deny us:*

2 Timothy 3:12. *12 Yea, and all that will live godly in Christ Jesus shall suffer persecution.*

1 Peter 2:20. *20 For what glory is it, if, when ye be buffeted for your faults, ye shall take it patiently? but if, when ye do well, and suffer for it, ye take it patiently, this is acceptable with God.*

1 Peter 3:14 - 18. *14 But and if you suffer for righteousness' sake, happy are you: and be not afraid of their terror, neither be troubled; 15 But sanctify the Lord God in your hearts: and be ready always to give an answer to every man that asks you a reason of the hope that is in you with meekness and fear: 16 Having a good conscience; that, whereas they speak evil of you, as of evildoers, they may be ashamed that falsely accuse your good conversation in Christ. 17 For it is better, if the will of God be so, that you suffer for well doing, than for evil doing. 18 For Christ also has once suffered for sins, the just for the unjust, that he might bring us to God, being put to death in the flesh, but quickened by the Spirit:*

1 Peter 4:15. *15 But let none of you suffer as a murderer, or as a thief, or as an evildoer, or as a busybody in other men's matters. –* <u>The reason we suffer</u>.

1 Peter 4:16, 19. *16 Yet if any man suffer as a Christian, let him not be ashamed; but let him glorify God on this behalf. 19 Wherefore let them that suffer according to the will of God commit the keeping of their souls to him in well doing, as unto a faithful Creator. –* <u>The attitude of a Christian towards suffering</u>.

178

Important Scriptures that demonstrates this teaching is: -

Philippians 4:11 - 14. *11 Not that I speak in respect of want: for I have learned, in whatsoever state I am, therewith to be content. 12 I know both how to be abased, and I know how to abound: every where and in all things I am instructed both to be full and to be hungry, both to abound and to suffer need. 13 I can do all things through Christ which strengthens me. 14 Notwithstanding you have well done, that you did communicate with my affliction.*

Philippians 4:16-19. *16 For even in Thessalonica you sent once and again unto my necessity. 17 Not because I desire a gift: but I desire fruit that may abound to your account. 18 But I have all, and abound: I am full, having received of Epaphroditus the things which were sent from you, an odour of a sweet smell, a sacrifice acceptable, wellpleasing to God. 19 But my God shall supply all your need according to his riches in glory by Christ Jesus.*

Why would the *world* like to cause us to suffer (it is <u>they</u> that will cause the suffering – directly and indirectly)? The answer is quite straightforward.

- They love darkness because their works are evil.
- We bring light into their world and it exposes them for who & what they are.
- They hate being accountable to anyone – especially to a God they cannot see.
- We cause guilt to rise up in them and they feel uncomfortable.
- They are jealous of the assurance that we have of eternal life and they know the alternative is hell – their destination.
- We represent a standard that they cannot achieve and therefore they will do their best to cause you to stumble and show that you are the *same as them*. What they do not realize is that the

difference is not physical, or even in the works you do, but is in fact a difference in your heart.
- To avoid accountability and submission to God, they try to pass the blame, deny God, find alternative belief systems and deceive themselves.
- And the satan[66] is close at hand to assist them in their endeavours.

As you will notice, it has nothing to do with what you have done, good or bad, but who you are in the Lord that they hate. They have gone to the extent that they have made laws to make the Saints guilty of something. Even to the point that we cannot practice our Bible teaching on a daily basis. Examples are the abortion laws, the *anti-smacking* laws, evangelism is being targeted, *evolution* is accepted as science and is a compulsory subject at school, sexual orientation in 5 year olds (among others) is a pressured subject, etc.

This all falls into the definition of the word and experience of *suffering*.

A Gem: -

When God asks a question, like when He asked Adam "Where are you?" in Genesis 3, He is not seeking information because He is Omniscient (all knowing). He already knows the answer. He is asking so that you can examine yourself and assess where you are in relation to Him and adjust yourself to line up with the Lord again (through repentance, or obedience, or whatever the action required is, to get you back into your relationship with Him.).

Chapter End Notes

51 This refers to the Scripture that gives us insight into the relationship between the Gentiles (non-Jews) and the Jewish family (Romans 11:17 – 27).

52 When Scripture speaks about the relationship between God and the Believers, it infers a *wedding* or a *marriage concept*. Jesus is called the "Bridegroom" and the Believers (Born-Again perhaps) are His "Bride" (Psalms 19:5; Isaiah 61:10; Jeremiah 7:34; Matthew 9:15; John 2:9; Revelation 18:23 and others) and perhaps some Jews (Messianic Jews).

There are Old Testament Saints as well as New Testament Saints. From the Jewish point of view, there are also *God Lovers*, which are Gentiles that love God (Acts chapter 10 and others) but were not proselytes (Matthew 23:15 and others). Then you get the enemies of the Bridegroom as well.

Some postulate that these different groups of people are all brought together and into context in the Marriage supper where Jesus is the Bridegroom, the Believers (also called the *Church*) is the Bride, the Jews are the family, the *God Lovers* are the friends, and the angels are the servants (as can be seen in the account of the *certain man* in Luke 14 [This is not a parable because the Bible always tells us when a parable is being told.]). The reasoning behind this is actually quite simple. If the *Body* or *True Church* is born at the arrival of the Holy Spirit (Acts 2) then the only way to be part of the True Church is to have the same experience. The disciples were "just" disciples until they were filled with the Holy Spirit; and even then, they did not fully understand this concept until Paul received the revelation of the True Church (found in Galatians). Peter claims that

Paul wrote *things difficult to understand* (2 Peter 3:16). This theory does not take into account the Hebrew definitions, words and meanings that, although similarly recognize the wedding theme, may not identify the parties involved in the same way.

The consideration, and the most important one, in my mind, would be the *True Church* or *Congregation* is made up of Born-Again, Spirit-filled, Saints and they are part of the *Body of Christ!* The Body of Christ and the *Church* or *Congregation* (which is the *Bride*) cannot be the same people. Those that are *Born-Again* and not filled with the Holy Spirit, may be *God Lovers* or as some call them, the *Church*, and may be part of the *Bride*. Today, even though the True Congregation is largely misunderstood from within and without, we still have a general idea of the marriage concept. And, because we have neglected or removed the Jewish flavour from the True Congregation, we have lost the understanding of the *marriage relationship* we have with God. It is interesting how the parallel is so accurate.

There is another consideration, the Word states that we are to be found *worthy* to be part of the rapture [Luke 20:35; 21:36]. Obviously, if one is not found *worthy*, they shall be left behind. Remember that being *worthy* is not to be confused with earning salvation, which we cannot do; it has to do with the *living works* that only the Holy Spirit can *quicken*, or *make alive*. There is more to this train of thought, but as this is not a study on the marriage relationship of the Lamb, I shall restrict myself to the comments just made.

53 As opposed to tongues used in public meetings and for the operation of the gifts of the Spirit.

54 The reference to the *point of contact* at any time here-
after is a reference to the human action that places
a demand upon the virtue of God. God has made
many promises to His people. He has also made
it abundantly clear that He expects His people to
practice *receiving* from the hand of God (in whatever
area the need may be). The *point of contact*, then, is
the point of faith that causes a withdrawal from the
"bank account" of heaven to be effected.

55 The Noahic covenant reaffirms the conditions of life
of fallen man as announced by the Adamic covenant,
and institutes the principle of human government
to curb the outbreak of sin, since the threat of divine
judgement in the form of another flood has been
removed. The elements of the covenant are:-

1 Man is made responsible to protect the sanctity
of human life by orderly rule over the individual
man, even to capital punishment (Genesis 9:5, 6;
compare Romans 13:1-7).

2 No additional curse is placed upon the ground,
nor is man to fear another universal flood
(Genesis 8:21; Genesis 9:11-16).

3 The order of nature is confirmed (Genesis 8:22;
Genesis 9:2).

4 The flesh of animals is added to man's diet
(Genesis 9:3, 4). Scripture tells us that man was a
vegetarian prior to the flood (Genesis 1:29 & 30).

5 A prophetic declaration is made that the
descendants of Canaan, one of Ham's sons, will
be servants to their brethren (Genesis 9:25, 26).

6 A prophetic declaration is made that Shem will
have a peculiar relation to the Lord (Genesis
9:26, 27). All divine revelation is through Semitic

men, and Christ, after the flesh, descends from Shem.

7 A prophetic declaration is made that from Japheth will descend the enlarged races (Genesis 9:27). Government, science, and art are the indisputable record of the exact fulfilment of these declarations.

56 The Holy Spirit, in the New Testament, summary:-

1 The Holy Spirit is revealed as a divine person. This is expressly declared (e.g. John 14:16, 17, 26; John 15:26; John 16:7-15; compare Matthew 28:19), and everywhere else implied.

2 The revelation concerning him is progressive:

(a) In the Old Testament He comes upon whom he will, apparently without reference to conditions in them.

(b) During His earth-life Christ taught through prayer to the Father.

(c) At the close of His ministry He promised that He would Himself pray to the Father, and in answer to His prayer the Comforter would come to abide (John 14:16,17).

(d) On the evening of His resurrection He came to the disciples in the upper room and breathed on them saying, "Receive the Holy Spirit (Ghost)" (John 20:22), but He instructed them to wait before beginning their ministry until the Spirit should come upon them (Luke 24:49; Acts 1:8).

(e) On the day of Pentecost the Spirit came upon the whole body of believers (Acts 2:1-4).

(f) After Pentecost the Spirit was imparted to such as believed, in some cases by the laying on of hands (Acts 8:17; Acts 9:17).

(g) With Peter's experience in the conversion of Cornelius (Acts10) it became clearer that the norm for this age was that the Jew and Gentile were saved on precisely the same conditions, and the Holy Spirit was to be given without delay to those who met the one essential condition of trust in Christ (Acts 10:44; Acts 11:15-18). The evidence for this conclusion rests on the fact that they began to glorify God in 'Tongues'. This is the permanent fact for the entire "Church age". Every believer is born of the Spirit (John 3:3-6; John 5:1); Indwelt by the same Spirit, whose presence makes the believer's body a temple (1 Corinthians 6: 19; compare Romans 8:9-15; Galatians 4:6; 1 John 2:27); and baptized with the Spirit (1 Corinthians 12:12,13; 1 John 2:20,27), thus sealing him for God (Ephesians 1:13; Ephesians 4:30).

3 The New Testament distinguishes between having the Spirit, which is true of all believers, and being filled with the Spirit which is the Christian's privilege and duty (compare Acts 2:4 with Acts 4:29-31; Ephesians 1:13, 14 with Ephesians 5:18). There is one baptism with the Spirit, but many fillings with the Spirit.

4 The Holy Spirit is related to Christ in his conception (Matthew 1:18-20; Luke 1:35), baptism (Matthew 3:16; Mark 1:10; Like 3:22; John 1:32, 33), walk and service (Luke 4:1, 14), resurrection (Romans 8:11), and as His witness throughout the age (John 15:26; John 16:8-11, 13, 14).

5   The Spirit forms the Church (Matthew 16:18; Hebrews 12:23, note) by baptizing all believers into the body of Christ (1 Corinthians 12:12,13; compare the universal address, 1 Corinthians 1:1,2); imparts gifts for service to every member of the body (1 Corinthians 12:7-11; 1 Corinthians 12:27-30); guides the members in their service (Acts 16:6,7); and is Himself the power of that service (Acts 1:8; Acts 2:4; 1 Corinthians 2:4).

6   The Spirit abides in a company of believers, making of them, corporately, a temple (1 Corinthians 3:16, 17).

7   The New Testament indicates a threefold personal relationship of the Spirit to the believer: "with", "in" and "upon" (John 14:16, 17; 1 Corinthians 6:19; Acts 1:8). "With indicates the approach of God to the soul, convicting of sin (John 16:9), presenting Christ as the object of faith (John 16:14), imparting faith (Ephesians 2:8), and regenerating (Mark 1:8; John 1:33). "In" describes the abiding presence of the Spirit in the Christian's body (1 Corinthians 6:19) to give victory over the flesh (Romans 8:2-4; Galatians 5:16,17), create the Christian character (Galatians 5:22,23), help infirmities (Romans 8:26), inspire prayer (Ephesians 6:18), give conscious access to God (Ephesians 2:18), actualize to the Christian his sonship (Galatians 4:6), apply the Scriptures in cleansing and sanctification (Ephesians 5:26; 2 Thessalonians 2:13; 1 Peter 1:2), comfort and intercede (Acts 9:31; Romans 8:26), and reveal Christ (John 16:14). "Upon" is used of the relationship on the Holy Spirit to the Lord Jesus Christ (Matthew 3:16; Mark 1:10; Luke 4:18; John 1:32,33), to the

virgin Mary in connection with the incarnation and birth of our Lord (Luke 1:35), to certain designated disciples (Luke 2:25 [Simeon]; Acts 10:44,45; Acts 11:15 [household of Cornelius]; Acts 19:6 [disciples at Ephesus]), and to believers generally (Luke 24:49; Acts 1:8; 2:17; 1 Peter 4:14).

8 Based on Luke 4:18, some understanding that the expression has to do with anointing for special service for God, as well as with the original coming and indwelling of the Holy Spirit to and in the individual Christian.

Sins against the Spirit, committed by unbelievers, are:

> To blaspheme (Matthew 12:31)
> Resist (Acts 7:51)
> Insult (Hebrews 10:29, "hath done despite").

Christian's sins against the Spirit are: -

> To grieve Him by allowing evil in heart or life (Ephesians 4:30,31)
> To quench Him by disobedience (1 Thessalonians 5:19).

The right attitude toward the Spirit is yieldedness to His sway in life, service, and constant willingness for Him to "put away" whatever grieves Him or hinders His power (Ephesians 4:31).

The symbols of the Spirit are: (a) oil (John 3:34; Hebrews 1:9); (b) water (John 7:38,39); (c) wind (John 3:8; Acts 2:2); (d) fire (Acts 2:3); (e) a dove (Matthew 3:16); (f) a seal (Ephesians 1:13;

Ephesians 4:30); and (g) an earnest, or pledge (Ephesians 1:14).

57 Agape – the God kind of Love – centred in sacrifice.

58 This stems from a knowledge of what God has done, or Who He is, that brings a sense of 'well-being' – ending in an emotion. It is not just an emotional happiness.

59 This is a definition of 'peace' that I was given and I would like to share here: - (A bird is sitting on a rock cliff. A herd of animals thunder in a panic, and causing mayhem, pounded the earth just below, in a mindless rush to *nowhere*. That bird was at true peace because it was not affected by the mayhem and panic from below.) The bird is not affected by outside *forces* and cannot be understood by the mind. The Hebrew word for *peace* is "Shalom" and literally means: - "Destroy the authority that binds us to chaos." This would include salvation, peace, healing, and so on. 'Chaos' being the dismantling of order and truth.

60 Longsuffering is not just being patient. It embraces taking evil acts against you and holding no grudges. It embraces the continued work with people who, not only show ungratefulness, but sometimes violently oppose you.

61 This is an attitude of "gentle answers turning away wrath" (Proverbs 15:1).

62 God would not ask us to do something beyond our ability. This would include: - fleeing the appearance of evil, being bold enough to be a role model, thinking and acting in a pure fashion, and so on.

63 This is the God kind of faith. The most faith you will ever need is in the act of being *Born-Again*. Yet

you need it while still a sinner. This is evidence that it is indeed a gift of God and comes from God alone.

64 Meekness is not weakness! A horse, powerful and wild can be ridden once 'broken', but it has not lost its power, speed or danger. It is now simply channelled or directed. Directing your life into God's will and your destiny is – meekness!

65 Temperance is softening your position in the actions you would like to take. It does not include compromise, but rather a 'gentler' judgement and patience in explaining the truth with the purpose (hope?) of repentance. Another word to describe *temperance* would be *self-control*.

66 The word "satan" is not the name of the devil. The word means "adversary, enemy, resistor, etc." So the word can be used for a system, person, idea, attitude, etc. because it is anything that resists the Word, works, person, purposes, etc. of God. Calling a devil or demon 'satan' is therefore acceptable. Calling a person that resists the works of God, 'satan', is acceptable. Jesus called Peter "satan" because he did not want Jesus to die on the cross (Matthew 16:23). (*23 But he turned, and said unto Peter, Get thee behind me, satan: thou art an offence unto me: for thou savourest not the things that be of God, but those that be of men.*)

But having said that, using it as a real name is quite acceptable too, because it identifies the head of the whole adversaries' army, which resists the Living God. You will find that even when I use the word as a name, I break grammatical rules by not capitalizing the name. I refuse to glorify the enemy of all

that is good in any way or form. he is not worthy of the honour of any respect whatsoever and I mention him in this book only because he is an entity that needs to be exposed, or his methods unveiled. If the word is capitalized at all, it is because it is a direct quote from another source, say, the Holy Bible.

Chapter 11

Laying on of Hands

Although the practice of laying on of hands is
nowhere taught (as a doctrine) in the Bible, we
learn of its existence and importance by the examples
we see in the Bible. Jesus does, however, command us
to practice it in the 'great commission'. Mark 16:15 - 18.
Bible characters, throughout the Bible, practised laying
on of hands. The Hebrew has a clear understanding of
this practice and does practice it often.

There is a Scripture that some use to indicate the
power of the Laying on of Hands. (Habakkuk 3:4 _And_
his brightness was as the light; he had horns coming out
of his hand: and there was the hiding of his power.) They
conclude that the power of God is 'hidden in His
(God's) hands'. When they lay hands on you they are
representing the Lord – you are His body on the earth,
and He (God) would honour the act of faith; which in
itself is right. The reason I am hesitant to accept this
thought outright is that I, personally, have not found
the second or third Scripture that says the same ("by
the witness of two or three. . .").

There are seven different reasons for *Laying on of Hands* found in the Bible.

They are: -

- For healing
- For receiving the baptism in the Holy Spirit
- For imparting gifts
- For ordaining into an office
- For release into ministry
- Bless children (even prophesy over your own children in faith)
- For identification with the subject person[67]

There is no *magical* power in Laying on of Hands. The last point, above, is actually the definition or reason for the Laying on of Hands. It is the *contact point* for the release of faith.

As an example for the contact point for the release of faith, we can look at the <u>*woman with the issue of blood*</u> in Luke.

Luke 8:43 - 47. *43 And a woman having an issue of blood twelve years, which had spent all her living upon physicians, neither could be healed of any, 44 Came behind him, and touched the border of his garment: and immediately her issue of blood stanched. 45 And Jesus said; Who touched me? When all denied, Peter and they that were with him said, Master, the multitude throng you and press [you], and you say, Who touched me? 46 And Jesus said, Somebody hath touched me: for I perceive that virtue is gone out of me. 47 And when the woman saw that she was not hid, she came trembling, and falling down before him, she declared unto him before all the people for what cause she had touched him and how she was healed immediately.*

She touched Jesus' clothes and was healed. The clothes did not heal her, nor did the touch of her hand. The virtue of Jesus healed her. But, the touch of the robe was the <u>contact point</u> for the release of faith and of God's power!

Just as an aside, the hem of a garment (of a king, or a priest, or a prophet, etc.,) was the mark of their authority or anointing.

> ➤ David cut off Saul's hem in the cave and became ashamed of his action [understanding this explains why he became ashamed].
> ➤ Aaron's robe and the priestly robes are described in Moses' writings (and other places), which all demonstrate the use of the hem as their authority.
> ➤ Somewhat like a policeman's badge.

<u>Notice</u>: All these principles are *soaked* in the application of <u>FAITH</u>! (*"Without faith it is impossible to please God"* (Hebrews 11:6) and *"What is not of faith is sin"* (Romans 14:23).) This makes your lifestyle, one of faith. Christians can live no other way – what a blessing!

Healing

Healing relies upon:

* Faith on the part of the minister, and/or
* Faith on the part of the sick, and/or
* A supernatural act of mercy by God.

But, the healing is <u>always</u> to the glory of God and <u>by</u> the power of the Holy Spirit. The laying on of hands is the <u>contact point</u> that releases the evidence of the power of God.

Why does Healing not Always Manifest Immediately?

Nowhere does God promise an immediate healing, rather He says that the healing process has begun: -

(James 5:15 *And the prayer of faith shall save the sick, and the Lord shall raise him up; and if he have committed sins, they shall be forgiven him.*).

The goodness of God usually manifests His healing immediately. There are times when God expects us to put our faith to the test. Not for Him to see if we have strong faith, but rather, for *us* to see how strong our faith really is. You see, we are often told to believe in God. Even in this book I have encouraged you to do so; but God believes in YOU!!! He believes you can grow; as well as be victorious over the enemy, circumstances, sickness, poverty, the world, etc. Now YOU need to see that you can. . .in other words, you need to see yourself as God sees you.

A quick healing is great and sometimes you need it. And, sometimes you need to mix your faith with God's promises to see the results, which is glorious and precious!

1 Peter 1:7 (*That the trial of your faith, being much more precious than of gold that perishes, though it be tried with fire, might be found unto praise and honour and glory at the appearing of Jesus Christ:*)!

Inner Healing

We are sometimes warned against 'inner healing' by misguided but well-meaning Saints. The reason for this is simple to understand. Some false religions use a similar practice to indulge in their pagan and occultic activities. We need to remember that the satan is a liar, a murderer and can only corrupt things; he cannot create or initiate anything, except sin. So he takes God's methods and corrupts them. Imagination is a God-given capability.

Inner healing involves you thinking about a past hurt and explaining it to the godly councillor with you. The godly councillor will ask you questions about the incident, and you would then have to picture the experience in your mind. It is in fact, calling up your past. It would not require a forced memory, but is a memory that you know about and which is giving you discomfort or pain. You will then be asked to see Jesus in the scene and see what He is doing.

Invariably, Jesus will be doing something that will comfort you. Then you will be prayed for and Jesus will be asked, by His Holy Spirit, to heal that hurt. The end result is that the experience remains a memory, but the 'sting' is removed and you will only think of it (in future) in passing; and it will not cause pain.

This should be done only with an experienced Godly Deliverance Minister as they know what questions to ask. But, it is simple, open and certainly not occultish.

Receiving the Holy Ghost

One cannot impart the Holy Ghost by the Laying on of Hands. The Laying on of Hands is only for encouragement to receive by <u>faith</u>. Only Jesus can Baptize in the Holy Ghost (Mark 1:7, 8). Again, it is the point of contact for the release of faith.

Imparting gifts

This is the only "imparting" that can be done by the laying on of hands. And then, it is God who imparts the gifts. We, in faith, and by the direction of the Holy Spirit, pray for the gifts to be imparted and rely on God to keep His Word of Promise. We do this while operating in the gifts of the Spirit (e.g. Word of Knowledge).

Ordaining into the Ministry

In many instances, this is actually to recognize that a person has been practising a certain office and now, we accept and recognize that he is filling that office. This includes giving him the title and rewards of that office, e.g. Evangelist.

People do not fill the office and *then* begin practising the requirements of that office. (Unless God supernaturally calls you to that office.) Few leaders approve of this experience because it is something they have no control over. Many become *permission withholders* at this point. I believe it is mainly because of their traditional training that they dislike recognizing that God is calling others to a certain ministry, and they have no say, or control, in the matter. They may have forgotten that the Congregation belongs to Jesus and it is *He* that shall build His Congregation (Matthew 16:18).

Release into Ministry

This is to "officially" release a person into a ministry outside of our Congregation environment. This is <u>only</u> after <u>God</u> calls them. (Whether or not anyone else agrees with that calling.) God does the calling and sending. We lay hands in recognition of this fact and release them with our love and blessing, by faith. It has to be *by faith* because sometimes we cannot understand God's choice of vessel.

Identification with the Subject Person

Human nature craves physical contact and this is the loving sign of our identification and promise of support. (Examples of support are: - blessing, provision, protection, guidance, support, encouragement, etc.) There is no physical guarantee that what we are praying for by the laying on of hands shall happen. The promises given in the Word of God are our only guarantee. The reason for this is that we must rely upon God and His grace to make it come to pass in the physical. We must believe it enough to act upon it and God will respond by working it out in the physical.

Chapter End Notes

67 A principle called *the identification principle* is being
taught by some and can be seen throughout the
teachings in this book.

Rabbit trail starts...

Chapter 12

Confession

B efore dealing with the next point, I need to deal
with a subject that is normally confused, or of
which people are ignorant. The subject is *Confession.*
In certain Churches (mostly falsely so claimed), they
teach that the only way to remove one's sin is to confess
your sin – true so far, but here is where they leave the
Biblical application – the confession is said to "have to
be made" to a *priest* or some such intermediary.

The truth is that when confession is made, it is to be
to the Lord alone – between you and Him. (Ezra 10:11
*Now therefore make confession unto the LORD God of your
fathers, and do his pleasure: and separate yourselves from
the people of the land, and from the strange wives.*) There
is no dire need, or conditional prerequisite for you to
confess to someone, to have your sins removed. I do
concede, however, that confessing one's sins to someone
(human), normally the person that has led you to the
Lord, does form a mentor/accountability relationship.
This is good and to be desired. But, that is only on a relationship basis, as opposed to a *requirement of salvation.*

Under *Conviction, Repentance,* and *Increasing Faith,* earlier, I touch on the subject of *Confession.* The implication is that you need to recognize your sin as *sin,* as opposed to a *problem* in your life. Telling God this, lines you up, in attitude, with the Word of God. This becomes conducive (helps along) to the salvation message.

A simple definition of *confession* is that we "need to say what God is saying on the subject."

But there is a Scripture that says that we need to confess our faults to one another (James 5:16 *Confess your faults one to another, and pray one for another, that you may be healed. The effectual fervent prayer of a righteous man avails much.*). I am glad you mentioned that!

This is speaking of relationships that are *father/son* type of relationships. Where we can speak freely of our "weaknesses" and get support to strengthen them. The word *faults* speaks of *weaknesses* and not *sin.* The type of relationship that I am describing here is found in a True Congregation of Saints.

Another aspect of confession is the fact that we must confess the receipt of our prayer requests, with thanksgiving. In fact, we need to be extremely careful with our tongues (what we say). Let us follow some Scriptures and see where they take us.

> Proverbs 18:20, 21. *²⁰A man's belly shall be satisfied with the fruit of his mouth; and with the increase of his lips shall he be filled. ²¹Death and life are in the power of the tongue: and they that love it shall eat the fruit thereof.*

Here we see that **_you_** have LIFE and DEATH in the power of your tongue. You need to be wise with what you say, from now on. As an example, should you keep telling someone that they are "useless" or some other untruth, that confession 'binds' that curse to them. But, if you keep telling them how 'clever' they are, that blessing follows them wherever they go!

Proverbs 21:23. [23]*Whoso keeps his mouth and his tongue keeps his soul from troubles.*

Proverbs 15:1 – 4. [1]*A soft answer turns away wrath: but grievous words stir up anger.* [2]*The tongue of the wise uses knowledge aright: but the mouth of fools pours out foolishness.* [3]*The eyes of the LORD are in every place, beholding the evil and the good.* [4]*A wholesome tongue is a tree of life: but perverseness therein is a breach in the spirit.*

Proverbs 13:2, 3. [2]*A man shall eat good by the fruit of his mouth: but the soul of the transgressors shall eat violence.* [3]*He that keeps his mouth keeps his life: but he that opens wide his lips shall have destruction.*

Luke 6:45. [45]*A good man out of the good treasure of his heart brings forth that which is good; and an evil man out of the evil treasure of his heart brings forth that which is evil: for of the abundance of the heart his mouth speaks.*

Then, of course there is James chapter three; which is much too long for me to type out here and discuss. So please read it and meditate (thing deeply about) on it.

Hebrews 13:15. [15]*By him therefore let us offer the sacrifice of praise to God continually, that is, the fruit of our lips giving thanks to his name.*

Think of this, if someone had to criticize you every day, how would you feel? I know of people that have committed suicide because they believed the negative things that were said about/to them, to the point that they saw no hope for the future. Yet I also know of people that, when complimented and praised for their efforts, achieved greatly against impossible odds.

Now that you have been made aware of the importance of words and how to use, or how not to use, them, let us link this subject to the next point. When one prays for you, or you pray for someone, what is said in the prayer could influence the recipient's attitude or faith to receive or not to receive the answer to the prayer.

You have the power to receive, for example, sickness by just saying, continually, how sick you are or feel. You can also, by the same token, resist the enemy of your soul by confessing your victory over him. He will have NO POWER over you simply because you *confessed* his impotence (powerless) in your life. You can resist him, bruise him, cast him out, overcome him and gain all sorts of victories over him, simply by saying, and believing, what you desire.

- ✓ I have been for deliverance, personally, and the team that prayed for me gained enormous victories for me in my life.
- ✓ I have also prayed for deliverance, on my own, and gained enormous victories too.
  - o The difference is simply that I had to know and believe the truth;
  - o I had to grow spiritually;
  - o I had to use my faith at the level that I was at – at that time;
  - o And I had to co-operate with the Holy Spirit in His dealing with me.

What I have shared with you now (confession), is a big *key* that you can use in your spiritual life to great effect.

Can there be problems when Laying on of Hands?

Another controversial subject is the **transference of spirits**.

There are only two types of *angel* and the angels all fall into a *hierarchy* that was set by the Lord when He created them. On the top or chief tier there are Cherubim, which is *in charge of* the lower tiers. The middle tier is the Seraphim and the lower tier is the Teraphim.

There are two types of *evil spirit*[68], the *devils* and the *evil beasts* (also called – among other things - *brute beasts* and *demons*). The reason there are *devils* and *demons* is that the *fallen angels* are the devils and the souls of what we call *nephilim* are the demons (the *devils* had sexual relations with women and produced *nephilim* which, when they died became the *demons*.)

Furthermore, you have the human spirit. But a human spirit is either: - in the human being, or in the *holding pen* (the KJV Bible calls it *hell*), or in the presence of God. (The evil spirits, demons, and devils I shall deal with as a subject in the *rabbit trails book*.)

If one type of angel (say, the righteous angel), can manifest themselves to humans (and *as* humans) and interact with humans (and they do on occasion), then these devils can do the same.

Before proceeding, I would like you to imagine an evil spirit as a bad *attitude*. This may help you *get your mind around* the subject of evil influence. An example of which, could be walking into a place where there is a depressive spirit. You would become depressed if you spent an appreciable period of time in its presence.

Demonology is a vast subject and can be depressing or unpleasant as well as VERY controversial. I shall sidetrack here for the purpose of understanding this subject a little, even though I would have chosen to have simply referred you to some excellent books on deliverance, etc.

Before leaving this train of thought, the satan and his minions, being adversaries, will cause everything they touch, or have to do with, to be reversed in nature[69]. So when abaddon, who was the *angel of life* reveals his true nature, he manifests as the angel of death. The satan, who was the angel that reflected God's glory and truth is now the father of all lies; when he speaks, it has to be a lie because there is no glory in lies and he is opposed to the Father of all truth.

It follows, therefore, that when laws are passed that call *good-evil* and *evil-good* they are influenced and promoted by the satan and his minions – one shall produce the fruit of the one that they serve. If you serve the Living God, you shall produce salt and light in your life. But if you serve the enemy, you shall produce lies and all manner of evil as a lifestyle. [Isaiah 5:20 *Woe unto them that call evil good, and good evil; that put darkness for light, and light for darkness; that put bitter for sweet, and sweet for bitter!*].

It is no more an issue of "is *abortion* or *euthanasia* acceptable?" or "should we accept all sexual *orientations*?" it is more to the point to ask: - "Who is **YOUR** Lord?" [Joshua 24:15 *And if it seem evil unto you to serve the LORD, choose you this day whom ye will serve; whether the gods which your fathers served that were on the other side of the flood, or the gods of the Amorites, in whose land ye dwell: but as for me and my house, we will serve the LORD.*]

Rabbit Trail Ends. . .

Chapter End Notes

68 The evil angels fall into the same style *hierarchy* as
the Angels that did not rebel.
69 Their previous beauty becomes ugliness, light
becomes darkness, etc.

Rabbit Trail Starts...

Chapter 13

Perhaps I should deal with this subject a little

L et us examine the history of evil spirits slightly. There is a distinction between demons, devils, evil spirits and other invisible apparitions. Because this is not a study on the subject, I shall only speak of demons that often manifest as certain evil spirits. I shall also not differentiate between them except by using the correct identification (names).

God created many angels to present holy worship to Himself. The *hierarchy* of angels consist of: -

- The Teraph (plural – Teraphim)
- The Seraph (plural Seraphim) and
- The Cherub (plural Cherubim) which is also called *Archangel/s*.

Angels have the ability to make one choice with their free wills, and that is on *how* to worship God. Over these angels, God created six *archangels* to lead all the angels in worship. The names of these archangels were Gabriel, Michael, Raphael and Uriel. The other two that rebelled against God had their identification totally removed by God. They are never named in any Biblical related books. Even the one we call *satan* and *lucifer* actually has no name. The name *lucifer* is actually a name given to him by the Babylonians because he was (originally) the one that reflected the light of God which when translated should be *son of the morning* or *morning star.*

Now, *satan* is actually a title, like *terrorist.* A person that is a terrorist is not named *Mr Terrorist.* His *title* or *job description* is that he is a terrorist. The word *satan* means *adversary;* so when the Hebrew referred to him, they said "Ha satan" which is "the satan" – his title. Simply because I need to refer to him occasionally, I shall refer to *the satan,* (as you may have already noticed) using this title.

So, calling any devil, nephilim[70] or demon *satan* is totally accurate because their aim is to oppose anything to do with the Living God. But it is not their name.

The second one that rebelled is now called *abaddon* who was originally the *cherub of life.* He is now what we call the *angel of death.* Because he is seldom spoken of, or considered, he can carry on surreptitiously (secretly) and is the last enemy to be defeated by Jesus (although his power was broken at the cross).

The satan, was created more beautiful than any of the other creatures thus far. He had all sorts of instruments 'built' into him (as it were, in place of inner organs). His covering was of all sorts of precious stone with all their colours and clarity. When he reflected God's glory, it must have been awesome to behold! Because of his beauty, he decided that he would make himself a throne and place it above that of the Lord's and receive worship as a god too. Being a created being, he could be in only one place at any one time (like any man). But, God, being the one and only omnipresent (present everywhere at the same time) One, knew his thoughts, and cast him out. They, the two cherubim that rebelled, had corrupted a third of God's angels (I believe they all came from the three *hierarchal* levels) and God had to cast them out too.

God, Who still wanted fellowship with intelligent, free agents, created the world, man and all things physical to achieve this purpose. As you can now understand, every person born on earth is being observed by the spiritual realm (firstly, by evil spirits assigned to them by the satan). God too has assigned an angel to each person born – we call them *guardian angels* – and requires these angels to counter the evil intended by the evil angels.

The *Teraph* angels can show themselves to humans in physical form (sometimes for extended periods). It is easy now to understand that the spiritual realm is more "real" than the physical. The goal of the devils is to fulfil the satan's goal of his 5 "I will's[71]". If he cannot kill you, he will steal from you. If he cannot steal from you, he will try to destroy you. If he fails in all those efforts, he will try to extract worship from you. If that fails, he will try to stop you worshipping God.

The satan's 5 "I will's": -

Isaiah 14:4, 9 – 15. 4 That you shall take up this proverb against the king of Babylon, and say, How has the oppressor ceased! the golden city ceased! 9 Hell from beneath is moved for you to meet you at your coming: it stirs up the dead for you, even all the chief ones of the earth; it has raised up from their thrones all the kings of the nations. 10 All they shall speak and say unto you, Are you also become weak as we? Are you become like unto us? 11 Your pomp is brought down to the grave, and the noise of your violins: the worm is spread under you, and the worms cover you. 12 How are you fallen from heaven, O Lucifer, son of the morning! how are you cut down to the ground, which did weaken the nations! 13 For you have said in your heart, I will ascend into heaven, I will exalt my throne above the stars of God: I will sit also upon the mount of the congregation, in the sides of the north: 14 I will ascend above the heights of the clouds; I will be like the most High. 15 Yet you shall be brought down to hell, to the sides of the pit.

Musical[72] instruments built into the satan and his beautiful covering that reflects God's glory and God's 5 "I will's": -

Ezekiel 28:12 - 19. 12 Son of man, take up a lamentation upon the king of Tyrus, and say unto him, Thus says the Lord GOD; You sealed up the sum, full of wisdom, and perfect in beauty. 13 You have been in Eden the garden of God; every precious stone was your covering, the sardius, topaz, and the diamond, the beryl, the onyx, and the jasper, the sapphire, the emerald, and the carbuncle, and gold: the workmanship of your tabrets and of your pipes was prepared in you in the day that you were created. 14 You are the anointed cherub that covered; and I have set you so: you were upon the holy mountain of God; you have walked up and down in the midst of the stones of fire. 15 You were perfect in your ways from the day that you were created, till iniquity was found in you. 16 By the multitude of your merchandise they have filled the midst of you with violence, and you have sinned:

therefore I will cast you as profane out of the mountain of God: and I will destroy you, O covering cherub, from the midst of the stones of fire. 17 Your heart was lifted up because of your beauty, you have corrupted your wisdom by reason of your brightness: I will cast you to the ground, I will lay you before kings, that they may behold you. 18 You have defiled your sanctuaries by the multitude of your iniquities, by the iniquity of your traffick; therefore will I bring forth a fire from the midst of you, it shall devour you, and I will bring you to ashes upon the earth in the sight of all them that behold you. 19 All they that know you among the people shall be astonished at you: you shall be a terror, and never shall you be any more.

I would like to quote here from a book by Thomas & Nita Horn: - *"FORBIDDEN GATES HOW GENETICS, ROBOTICS, ARTIFICIAL INTELLIGENCE, SYNTHETIC BIOLOGY, NANOTECHNOLOGY, and HUMAN ENHANCEMENT HERALD THE DAWN OF TECHNODIMENSIGNAL SPIRITUAL WARFARE.*), because they say what I want to say so succinctly [completely & clearly] that I could not do better. Also, I agree completely with their comments and I believe I would be doing you a disservice by not pointing it out to you.

The Quote runs thus: -

Given the content of the previous chapter and the inevitability during the study of spiritual warfare that the thorny (if not polarizing) question will arise concerning whether true Christians can become demon possessed, we need to state unequivocally at this juncture that although *daimonizomai* ("to be demonized") and *echon daimonion* ("having a demon") are manifested within institutionalized Christianity, it is our belief that those who are truly born again can never actually be *possessed*—as in *inhabited*—by demons. There are numerous reasons for this conclusion, not the least of which is that there are no instances of "possession" of believers anywhere in the Bible. Not a single verse in the Scripture even warns of the possibility, and there are zero examples in the life of Jesus Christ and the early church of demons being cast out of Christians.

What we do find in Scripture regarding the inner space of believers is that our body *"is the temple of the Holy Ghost, which is in you, which ye have of God, and ye are not your own"* (1 Corinthians 6:19). In fact, John writes that *"he that is begotten of God, keepeth himself, and that wicked one toucheth him not"* (1 John 5:18). Therefore, *"What communion hath light with darkness? And what concord hath Christ with Belial? And what agreement hath the temple of God with idols? for ye are the temple of the living God; as God hath said, 'I will dwell in them; and I will be their God, and they shall be my people'"* (2 Corinthians 6:14b—16). These and similar Scriptures verify for those who have the Holy Spirit residing within them that they are positively redeemed and sealed from the torment of diabolical possession. As John also certified, "If the Son therefore shall make you free, ye shall be free indeed" (John 8:36).

Though in recent years, burgeoning "Christian deliverance ministries" have suggested otherwise, claiming that *daimonizomai* and *echon daimonion* infer the Lord's body can actually be inhabited by demons, it is usually a

211

matter of semantics. Confusion over the meaning of the terms "possession" and "demonization" is somewhat understandable from an exegetical standpoint, especially given how *daimonizomai* is used in Scripture to refer to a variety of problems and demonic manifestations. But because it is dangerous to promote precise definitions where none exist in Scripture, it should be noted that the actual phrase "demon possession" does not even appear in the Bible (Josephus coined this phrase near the end of the first century), and what some teachers classify as "possession" is actually demonization—a spirit from an external posture gains control or influence over a person. As such, literal possession is different than demonization, and ample evidence exists in the New Testament to conclude that whereas believers may never be "possessed," they most certainly can be tempted, influenced, oppressed, and even demonized by evil supernaturalism. To this end, the apostle Paul warned the Christians at Ephesus (Ephesians 4:25-31) not to give "place" (Greek: *topos*) to the devil, meaning a foothold, opportunity, power, occasion for acting, or doorway into one's personal space through which demonic strongholds can be established. Paul even listed particular behaviors that could lead to this fiendish union— lying, anger, wrath, stealing, bitterness, clamor, evil speaking (Greek *blasphemia:* "to blaspheme, gossip, slander others"), and malice. Elsewhere in the Bible, we learn that doorways for agents of Satan to enter a believer's life can also include encumbrances like fear, such as the fear that led Peter to deny Christ in Luke chapter 22 and that Jesus made clear was an effort by Satan to cause Peter to stumble (v. 31), and greed—as illustrated in the story of Ananias and Sapphira in Acts chapter 5, where "Satan" (v. 3) filled the couple's hearts to lie and to hold back a portion of money. Demonization of a Christian through these and similar weaknesses is usually gradual, where small decisions are made over an extended period of time during which the individual gives in to temptation, followed by ongoing and progressive surrender of territory within the mind and finally the flesh. Such steps to demonization may be summarized accordingly:

Temptation: The enemy discovers a weakness and appeals to it.

Influence: The individual entertains the idea and finally gives in to temptation. A foothold is established in the person's life, making it harder to resist the same or related activity in the future.

Obsession: The activity eventually becomes an unhealthy preoccupation and irresistible impulse leading to critical degrees of control over the individual. The power to resist is practically gone.

Demonization: Control over the individual by external power becomes substantial. What at one time was considered sinful and to be avoided is now an addiction. The person may no longer even recognize the tendency as immoral, and little or no fortitude to cease participating in the activity remains.

Possession: This can occur if the individual turns his or her back on God so as to fully embrace carnality, surrendering the body and mind to Satan's control. The desire to resist invasion by discarnate supernaturalism is vacated.

What immediately stands out in these steps and doorways to demonization is how central the mind of man is to the functioning battleground where spiritual warfare takes place. Whether it is lying, anger, wrath, stealing, bitterness, clamor, evil speaking, malice, fear, greed, or another human frailty, the battle begins in our thought life where we are tempted to give in to sin. "That's where Satan can manipulate people toward his ends discreetly and invisibly," writes Chip Ingram in *The Invisible War*. "If he can distort our thoughts, our emotions, and our knowledge, then our behaviors and relationships will fall the way he wants them to. And even if he doesn't manage to turn us to overt evil, a little bit of distorted thinking can neutralize us and render us practically ineffective."[16] In other words, if Satan cannot possess or demonize an individual, he will settle for what he can get, influencing the mind and spirit to whatever extent he can, keeping people ineffective or causing them to become a problem for their families, their communities, or their churches.

End of Quote.

Rabbit Trail Ends. . .

Can there be problems when laying on of Hands? (Part 2)

Imagine for a moment that you enter a room at a funeral. The sadness and depression will "come upon" you too. The depression could be likened to a demon oppressing you. As the depression takes hold, you can understand how a demon can influence you. They attempt to influence your judgement and your decision-making processes.

Should a person praying with you be influenced by a *spirit of lust* (for example), it may try to influence you in the same way too. This is called "transference of spirits". It sounds terrible and is misunderstood by many.

Some go to extremes by searching "behind every bush" to eradicate them. Some, going to the opposite extreme, ignore them and even doubt their influence or existence. The one gives too much credence to them, and the other may have fallen into one of the oldest traps of all.

That trap is denying that the satan and/or his minions exist, which in turn releases the satan to work in their life unhindered; because that person is not prepared to acknowledge the enemy's potential influence. Thus, the enemy enjoys impunity when/if he influences that person's decisions/life.

There is a situation where a person laying hands upon you may possibly transfer an evil spirit to influence you instead of the transfer of anointing. Why and how? Should the person praying for you be influenced by, have, be operating with, a demonic spirit, he could pass it to you if you are susceptible to it. What I mean by that is that God knows what is in your heart and will allow whatever you are already open to, or truly desire.

Jeremiah 17:10. *10 I the LORD search the heart, I try the reins, even to give every man according to his ways, and according to the fruit of his doings.*

Hebrews 4:12-13. *12 For the word of God is quick, and powerful, and sharper than any twoedged sword, piercing even to the dividing asunder of soul and spirit, and of the joints and marrow, and is a discerner of the thoughts and intents of the heart. 13 Neither is there any creature that is not manifest in his sight: but all things are naked and opened unto the eyes of him with whom we have to do.*

2 Thessalonians 2:11. *11 And for this cause God shall send them strong delusion, that they should believe a lie:*

Let me use the example of a religious spirit. It is an evil spirit that can operate even when there is an *Anointing of God* present. Many people are religious, and may not necessarily be Christian. Acting religiously from a religious heart attitude (thinking you're right) is an open door for a religious spirit (a typical sign of its presence is that the person displays the trait of not being teachable).

Now, the question arises: "Can a Christian have a devil or an evil spirit?"

Many men of God have argued, and produced Scriptures, to back-up their arguments for, and against, this possibility. As Tom and Nita Horn have already said (in the quote above), the Believer can only be influenced by what they are already weak in and the enemy takes full advantage of that weakness. The Believer cannot be demon possessed, but they can *possess* a demon. The demonic force can attack, influence, etc., the body and the soul of the Believer and, no, they cannot enter them in the truest sense; they cannot enter the spirit of the man.

That is the right and domain of the Spirit of God! The enemy gives sickness to the body if you allow it, and wounds the soul if you do not protect your mind. But can only influence the spirit by *remote-control*. To illustrate this point, look at the illustration below and imagine it as a pond of water. Should you cast a stone into the pond; the water will ripple over the entire pond, and thus "affect" the centre, the spirit. The Bible refers to it as "fiery darts" because it can only influence *from a distance*.

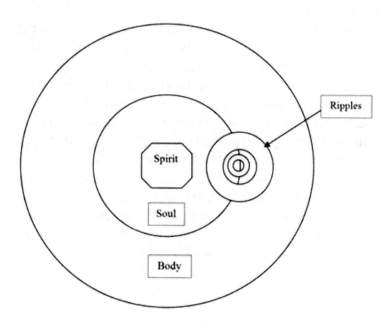

Strongholds are also built in the life of a Believer. The enemy takes months, even years to build these strongholds. But one prayer from a Child of God destroys it in seconds. Motorcars, washing machines, and the like, can be *automatic*. But salvation, the receiving of the Holy Spirit, deliverance, healing, and other benefits of the Child of God are not automatic (when you accept Jesus into your life, you are not automatically delivered, etc.).

They all need to be received as a gift from the Lord our God. (See Deuteronomy 18:9-13; Deuteronomy 28; Exodus 20:5, 34:7; and Numbers 14:18.)

What am I saying here? Do you need to fear the laying on of hands? That there is a demon lurking around waiting for you so that it can *jump onto/into you*? That you must be wary of Children of God praying for you?

You do not need to fear the laying on of hands at all. There are demons about, and they want desperately to relive the *human emotions*, and they are attacking the Children of God constantly, but they are not to be taken into account. If you are aware of them and choose to set your mind on Jesus, and obey Him at every opportunity, there will be no opening for any evil spiritual activity. And yes, you need to know that the person praying for you is demonstrating the nature and fruit of the Spirit of the Lord. Test it with your own spirit and do not be shy to avoiding even the ministry of such a person if your spirit has a *check* (which normally manifests in the loss of your peace). It may be a spirit of pride, lust, jealousy, etc., or simply a religious spirit that could be passed on. You do not want it, nor do you want it influencing your life and decision making processes.

Depending upon your attitude towards this subject, you would apply this Scripture to the situation (some more than others) Luke 11:9-13. When you are standing on God's Word, the Lord will ensure that no evil comes near you. Psalms 91: 1 – 7. [*1 He that dwells in the secret place of the most High shall abide under the shadow of the Almighty. 2 I will say of the LORD, He is my refuge and my fortress: my God; in him will I trust. 3 Surely he shall deliver you from the snare of the fowler, and from the noisome pestilence. 4 He shall cover you with his feathers, and under his wings shall you trust: his truth shall be your shield and buckler. 5 You shall not be afraid for the terror by night; nor for the arrow that flies by day; 6 Nor for the pestilence that walks in darkness; nor for the destruction that wastes at noonday. 7 A thousand shall fall at your side, and ten thousand at your right hand; but it shall not come nigh you.*]

Those that do not believe that a Christian can have a devil/demon influencing you are theoretically correct. Because they assume that all new Christians are taught correctly, are mature as soon as they are born again, and willing to cast off habits immediately! It would be great if that were so. But unfortunately, we do not live in a perfect world. Even those that believe that you are immediately delivered from all demonic influence, are still subject to bouts of depression, discouragement, criticism, gossiping, and so on; and maybe even being unteachable, which are all signs of demonic influence.

This may seem like a big negative in your life. NO, it is NOT. When an athlete builds muscle, he adds weights to his daily exercise routine. These attacks are there to help you build your faith, confession skills, etc. We all want "Great Victories" in our lives. But how do you achieve this without a "Great Battle"?

John 16:33 says: – These things I have spoken unto you, that in me ye might have peace. **In the world ye shall have tribulation: but** be of good cheer; **I have overcome the world**[73].

Doctrine of Baptisms & Laying on of Hands

Putting these two principles together, we see it as the lifestyle of the believer. Both of dying to self, and living only by faith (or *trust*); that is: allowing Jesus to live in you and you becoming the temple of the Holy Ghost. "I must decrease and He must increase." It is a lifestyle of living one with another in love and harmony – this takes FAITH (or *trust* [in the **Lord**, of course]).

The living with one another is called *fellowship*. An analogy is 'living like two FELLOWs in a SHIP = FELLOWSHIP'. Living together, tolerating one another and building unity and love (as a congregation) is another goal of our Lord! The Laying on of Hands is a picture of this principle.

Fill yourself with the Word of God and the presence of the Holy Spirit and you will leave no room for anything else – a full vessel can hold no more.

Become so *heaven conscious* that you become no use to the satan and his minions.

Chapter End Notes

70 The Teraphim, in this case the ones that *fell*, saw that the *daughters of men were fair*, they went in to them and lay with them (Genesis 6:1 – 5). The result was the off-spring called *nephilim*. When these nephilim died, and because they were not God's creation, their souls [they had no spirits from God] were left to wander the earth. These souls are referred to as *demons*. They strive to experience life on earth once again (as a human) and can only do so by inhabiting, or co-habiting, a human being. Even though the dead nephilim are *souls*, we refer to them as evil *spirits* and this is purely for convenience sake.

71 The satan's 5 "I will's" are found in Isaiah 14:13, 14. God responds with 5 "I will's" of His own, counteracting the satan's "I will's". They are found in Ezekiel 28:16 – 19.

72 Armed with this understanding, I am sure that you can grasp the ease with which he could use *backward masking* to embed his evil messages in popular music. And yes, he does. But this is a topic for a *rabbit trail* in a later book

73 Emphasis mine.

Chapter 14

Resurrection from the dead

There are three applications in this principle.
One is past; because Jesus rose, he demonstrated that future resurrections are possible. Jesus also caused all the Believers that had died before His death & resurrection to rise and accompany Him to their Heavenly dwelling place. [*Matthew 27:52, 53. 52 Also the graves were opened, and the bodies of many saints who had died were raised to life; and after Jesus rose, they came out of the graves and went into the holy city, where many people saw them.*]

One is futuristic; that is when we will be raised from the dead if we die before Jesus' return. [Romans 6:4, 5. 4 Therefore we are buried with him by baptism into death: that like as Christ was raised up from the dead by the glory of the Father, even so we also should walk in newness of life. 5 For if we have been planted together in the likeness of his death, we shall be also *in the likeness* of *his* resurrection:]

The Last One is in the present. The one that is present (because you are not dead yet) refers to the lifestyle we are living right now. [Romans 12:2 And be not conformed to this world: but be ye transformed by the renewing of your mind, that ye may prove what *is* that good, and acceptable, and perfect, will of God.]

The application also applies as follows: -

1 Our Spirits are resurrected when we are *Born-Again.*
2 Our Souls are resurrected as we renew them by the "washing of the Word."
3 Our Body shall be resurrected when Jesus returns to harvest His Children.

Resurrection means *to return life to what has died.*

Adam walked with God on a daily basis. This is the relationship that we have a right to as Children of God. Because he sinned, we have lost this relationship. When we accept Jesus as Lord and Saviour, this relationship is restored. The difference is that we need to learn how to walk with the Lord daily. This is what I refer to as the *present resurrection.*

This resurrection is to motivate us to obedience and action. Our whole Christian life depends upon our resurrection power. This power is available only by the baptism of the Holy Spirit. Because the Holy Spirit raised Jesus from the dead He will raise us up too. It is the Holy Spirit that will lead us into all truth.

Dead as we saw earlier was both *deceased* and *useless* or *unprofitable.* So, should you die, Jesus will raise you up because He rose! The application to us that are alive is that Jesus gives life and purpose to our useless or unprofitable lives.

This can and does mean:

- You will never die
- Your spirit will open your soul and body to eternal life as you study Scripture
- Your works will be given life because of your Godly attitudes (not dead works any more).

This gives encouragement and hope to the weakest Christian. Thus they are "resurrected" (in heart and mind) into the "Saints" that our God has already made them (actually)!

There are two future resurrections. The one is for Saints, (born-again believers), and the other is for the sinners. The one is to rewards and the other is to damnation.

The Resurrection of the Believers.

1 Corinthians 13:13. *13 And now there abides faith, hope, charity [love], these three; but the greatest of these is charity [love].*

This Scripture means, simply put, that after all our cares, processes and aspects of life; temporal and eternal, having been sifted and strained, only these three attributes will remain eternal.

'Faith' which is the action part of all life and existence.

'Hope' which is the goal, aim, or reason for living.

'Love' which is the motivation or substance for that life.

In relation to this principle Scripture, the *hope* of the believer is the resurrection. The Believer's hope is not a hit-and-miss "hope it will rain this week" type of hope.

It is the "Jesus rose from the dead and promised that I shall too" type of hope. It is a hope that is certain! Not an "if" hope but a "when" hope. It is part of our inheritance. If I should say: "I am hoping for tomorrow", that does not mean that tomorrow may, or may not, come. It means that I am looking forward to the break of day with anticipation.

Romans 5:2. *2 By whom also we have access by faith into this grace wherein we stand, and rejoice in hope of the glory of God*

Ephesians 1:18. *18 The eyes of your understanding being enlightened; that you may know what is the hope of his calling, and what the riches of the glory of his inheritance in the saints,*

Colossians 1:27. *27 To whom God would make known what is the riches of the glory of this mystery among the Gentiles; which is Christ in you, the hope of glory:*

1 Peter 1:21. *21 Who by him do believe in God, that raised him up from the dead, and gave him glory; that your faith and hope might be in God.*

The Believers <u>shall</u> be raised from the dead as sure as Jesus did! They shall be raised to receive rewards for their life's actions, attitudes and work!

Many get confused about the *End Times* because they do not realize that there is a difference between the *Rapture* and *Jesus' Second Coming*.

❖ God shall allow an Angel to sound a Trumpet and call with a *Loud Voice* and the dead in

Christ shall rise first and then we, who are still alive, shall be changed and *snatched* (raptured) from the earth to meet the Lord in the air. (1 Thessalonians 4:17.)

❖ And, with the Second Coming, Jesus puts His foot on the *Mount of Olives* and the earth splits. (Zechariah 14:4.)

❖ If we tried to combine these events, it would become confusing.

The Resurrection of the Unbelievers

This is actually a short, and not-so-sweet, subject. The unbeliever will also be resurrected. But he will only be raised from the dead on the day that the Lord sits upon His *Great White Throne*. This is also the day that they will answer for their rejection of Jesus and His efficacious Sacrifice. They will then go straight to the damnation that the Lord had created for the devil and his angels. So, theirs is best dealt with in the next section. . .Eternal Judgement.

Matthew 25:41. 41 *Then shall he say also unto them on the left hand, Depart from me, you cursed, into everlasting fire, prepared for the devil and his angels:*

Revelation 20:10-15. 10 *And the devil that deceived them was cast into the lake of fire and brimstone, where the beast and the false prophet are, and shall be tormented day and night for ever and ever. 11 And I saw a great white throne, and him that sat on it, from whose face the earth and the heaven fled away; and there was found no place for them. 12 And I saw the dead, small and great, stand before God; and the books were opened: and another book was opened, which is the book of life: and the dead were judged out of those things which were written in the books, according to their works. 13 And the sea gave up the dead which were in it; and death and hell delivered up the dead which were in them: and they were judged every man according to their works. 14 And death and hell were cast into the lake of fire. This is the second death. 15 And whosoever was not found written in the book of life was cast into the lake of fire.*

I need to sound a warning to the unbeliever (especially) and the believer alike. **Don't be fooled! You (everyone) shall stand before the Judge one day.**

- You may hide your head beneath the sand (metaphorically).
- You may accept evolution (modern man's tool for excusing himself from admitting to there being a God).
- You may try intimidation, swearing and violence against this message!
- You may believe in some idol, church, person or system.

But, you will still have to answer to the Judge!! – There is no way around this event!

Other Resurrections

There were and shall be other resurrections that I have not dealt with because they are not pertinent at this point of our study. I would, however, like to mention two more resurrections that you may come across during your daily Bible reading.

The first is one that has already taken place. It happened the day Jesus rose from the dead.

> Matthew 27:52, 53. *52 And the graves were opened; and many bodies of the saints which slept arose, 53 And came out of the graves after his resurrection, and went into the holy city, and appeared unto many.*

The second concerns those that died as martyrs during the *Tribulation Period*. These are those that die because they refuse to bow to the antichrist and are beheaded because of their stand.

> Revelation 20:4. *4 And I saw thrones, and they sat upon them, and judgment was given unto them: and I saw the souls of them that were beheaded for the witness of Jesus, and for the word of God, and which had not worshipped the beast, neither his image, neither had received his mark upon their foreheads, or in their hands; and they lived and reigned with Christ a thousand years.*

The faithfulness of our Father is unparalleled and as we understand more of His goodness, the more confident we can feel. And we can see, as we consider these Scriptures, the power that is available in His Holy Spirit – Bless His Name!

Chapter 15

Eternal Judgement

*E*ternal means *without end*. *Judgement* means *to balance, as in a scale, and render true and deserved rewards.* We always think of sending people to hell when we think of *judgement*.

But this has never been God's plan. Hell was prepared for the devil and his angels, not for man. But, through rebellion, man has chosen to follow the satan into hell.

Matthew 25:41 Then shall he say also unto them on the left hand, Depart from me, you cursed, into everlasting fire, prepared for the devil and his angels:

There are two judgements that we will look at right now. They are:

- Judgement of punishment
- Judgement of rewards

This subject also includes the resurrection; of which there are two. The first is the resurrection of the *redeemed* and the second is the resurrection of the *damned*.

The resurrection of the *redeemed* includes the *rapture*[74]. 1 Thessalonians 4:16. Whereas the resurrection of the *damned* is at the *Great White Throne*. Revelation 20:11.

What is the result of the Judgement of the damned?

- ➤ Being cast into the eternal hell fire (Matthew 18:8, 9)
- ➤ Eternal separation from God (2 Thessalonians 1:9, 10)
- ➤ The second death (Revelation 20:14, 15)
- ➤ Joining the devil and his angels (Matthew 25:41)
- ➤ Being in eternal punishment (Matthew 25:46)
- ➤ Being in darkness [with weeping & gnashing of teeth] (Matthew 25:30)
- ➤ Being shamed and in eternal contempt (Daniel 12:2)

What is the Believer's Judgement?

This is when the Believer's works will be tried by fire and the rewards will be given for what remains. (Revelation 3:18; 1 Peter 1:7; 1 Corinthians 3:13 - 15.)

Believers will receive rewards.

- ❖ A crown for leading others into righteousness (Daniel 12:3)
- ❖ A crown of righteousness (2 Timothy 4:7, 8)
- ❖ An everlasting crown (1 Corinthians 9:24, 25)
- ❖ A crown of life (James 1:12)
- ❖ A crown of glory (1 Peter 5:1 - 4)

There are also treasures in heaven for you (Matthew 6:19, 20. *19 Lay not up for yourselves treasures upon earth, where moth and rust does corrupt, and where thieves break through and steal: 20 But lay up for yourselves treasures in heaven, where neither moth nor rust does corrupt, and where thieves do not break through nor steal:*), which you need to send on ahead.

The Sheep & Goat Judgement

There is a judgement coming, and I do not want to go into when it will happen, but be assured it will happen. This is the judgement spoken of in Matthew 25:31 – 46. I shall just quote a few verses for the purpose of this comment.

(Matthew 25:31 – 34, 41, 46. 31 When the Son of man shall come in his glory, and all the holy angels with him, then shall he sit upon the throne of his glory: 32 And before him shall be gathered **all nations**: and he shall **separate them** one from another, as a shepherd divideth *his* **sheep from the goats**: 33 And he shall set the **sheep on his right** hand, but the **goats on the left**. 34 Then shall the King say unto them on his right hand, **Come**, you blessed of my Father, **inherit the kingdom** prepared for you from the foundation of the world: 41 Then shall he say also unto them on the left hand, **Depart** from me, **you cursed**, into everlasting fire, prepared for the devil and his angels: 46 And these shall go away into **everlasting punishment**: but the righteous into life eternal.)

This sounds harsh, and indeed it is, but let us look at why and what the judgement is for and who is it against.

If you turn to the Bible and look up this verse, you will notice that it has to do with the treatment of Jesus by the NATIONS. The individual may say "But when did I. . ." and then quote what Jesus uses to *measure* the nations' response to Him. "I was hungry, and you gave me meat: I was thirsty, and you gave me drink – and so on. . ." and you too may ask "but when did I. . ."

Look at Jesus' answer: - ". . .Inasmuch as you did *it* not to one of the least of these, ye did *it* not to me." Jesus was saying that because you did or did not do any of these considerations for the Jews, you did/did not do them for Him. There are other Scriptures to reinforce this thought, but the point is that the *brethren* of Jesus are the *yard-stick* here.

Depending upon your attitude toward the Hebrew in these last days, will determine your reward in this judgement.

> ➢ If you provided for,
> ➢ supplied to,
> ➢ supported,
> ➢ loved,
> ➢ befriended
> ➢ or any other beneficial action towards the Israeli today.
>> o Jesus will welcome you into your reward.
>> o But if you withhold or have an aggressive or belligerent attitude toward the Israeli today.
>>> ▪ you shall reap your rewards for your lack of love and support.

I have recently read of how the United Nations "Human Rights Lobby" is promoting punishment for companies trading with Israel and want the workers to be prosecuted for supporting the Hebrew nation. Where is the "Human Rights" of the Hebrews?

They have always had the land they are living in, and MORE! By divine covenant! Look at Genesis 17:8, Isaiah 61:7 and others. I quote just one Scripture, and notice please the word "everlasting". Genesis 48:4 (*And said unto me, Behold, I will make you fruitful, and multiply you, and I will make of you a multitude of people; and will give this land to your seed after you for an everlasting possession.*)

During the six-day war, and others, where was the United Nations when the aggressors attacked the fledgling nation? But when it appeared that Israel was about to totally defeat these nations (6 at-a-time) the United Nations quickly called a stop to it.

Today, there is a clear line being drawn between those supporting Israel and those opposing Israel so that when God's judgement comes, no-one can say "but I didn't know". There was no such thing as *Palestine*; this is a creation of the U.N. The name is based on an edict by the Romans designed to insult the Jews. The mohammadans (looking at the predominant religion in the nations surrounding Israel today) have NEVER possessed the land that Israel now possesses. No-one wanted the land until the Jews began returning to this land, and the quran does not even mention Jerusalem even once, as an important city. They have no claim to the land now and they have never had a claim to it. Their goal in claiming this is solely to have the Israelis destroyed, and the U.N. is a willing accomplice. If I had something to do with the U.N., I would quickly withdraw! It is a terrible judgement they are about to face.

Believers must give an Account

- ❖ For what we have done in their body
- ❖ Secrets will be exposed
- ❖ It will be done individually and,
- ❖ Before the throne of Jesus Christ

Looking at each judgement, we find that with the first judgement (judgement of the unbeliever), the judgement is based on what we did with the sacrifice of Jesus. If we reject Him, we will get punished because our sin killed Jesus. (Our sin nature killed Jesus, making us murderers of Jesus; which in turn makes our good, or bad, works ineffective either way. i.e. our good works cannot save us and our bad works cannot further condemn us.)

And with the second (the judgement of the Believers), Christians will receive rewards, based upon what we have done with the Holy Spirit, who differentiates between all our works being *living* or *dead* works.

Other (erroneous) teachings on Judgement

(1) Annihilation. i.e. There is nothing at the end (Hebrews 9:27).
(2) Punishment for a while; then annihilation (2 Corinthians 5:6 - 9).
(3) Universal reconciliation: here even the devil will be saved (Both above Scriptures render this possibility foolishness. Revelation 20:10; Matthew 25:31 - 46; Mark 9:47, 48).
(4) There are those desiring to justify their sin by hiding behind a warped train of thought that runs something like this: -

i. "God is a God of love, He will not judge us and send us to hell!" They "know not the power of God nor the Scriptures" (Mark 12:24). God is indeed a God of love.

ii. But, He is also a just God. He will indeed treat the sinner as a sinner and a Saint as a Saint. The sinner will indeed be banished to hell along with the greatest sinner that has been created – the satan!

iii. Furthermore, man would want it no other way. Justice must be equal and holiness must be equal with no grey areas.

Personally, I am amazed that so many people would listen to spewers of false doctrine and take comfort in those false doctrine. Rather than following the true, honest, and wholesome doctrine of the Living God, Who wants only their good. [I am referring here to those immersed in a false religion, claiming to be *Christian*.] How these deceived ones can prefer man's wisdom, and ultimate deception, to God's Word is a mystery to me. (But then again, I suppose that is why it is called *deception*.)

I believe the Word of God and see God's *proofs* everywhere. I recognize them as such and therefore give Him glory for them. They, on the other hand, claim to study the same Bible but choose to be deceived. I do deal with *proofs* in my *Rabbit Trails Book*, but they are only proof to **honest** observers {unbelievers or Believers}.

A Deeper Look at Judgement

Numbers in Scripture always carry significance. I would like to point out the number two and explain a few things concerning *two* and judgement. According to Scripture, two stands for division, separation and difference. This difference could be for good or for evil. As the Lord has given the number one the significance of unity or singularity.

The correlation between one and two can be seen in the God-ordained marriage. It begins with a man and a woman being separate and divided. In marriage, they become one and in the eyes of the Lord, there is a unity and a single person – as in Genesis 2:7, 18, 21 – 24; 1:27 where we see the creation of Adam and Eve. In creation, God created Adam and ". . .male and female He created them. . ." God did in fact create Eve at the same time He created Adam.

Eve was within Adam and the Lord removed her from his side (even as the *Bride of Christ* was born or created from the side of Jesus the Messiah when the spear was thrust into His side to confirm that He had died, paying the price for our sin). So the unity became divided into two separate ones. They would then come together in marriage and produce offspring who then would marry and produce offspring or seed. And so it went on until today where two can still become one in marriage and produce Godly seed.

When we die now, we are separated from our bodies; our one becomes *separated* and becomes two[75]. And this is the explanation at which I am driving.

There is as an example: -

> ➢ Male and female
> ➢ Jew and gentile
> ➢ Spiritual and physical
> ➢ Sperm (seed) and egg
> ➢ Body and soul (forming animal life or "brute beasts" [2 Peter 2:12; Jude 1:10]. This would

also apply to humans when their spirits are still unregenerated.)

➤ Life (consisting of soul & body [i.e. "brute beasts"] on the one hand) and spirit (which indicates eternal life by virtue of being *Born-Again* on the other hand)

➤ And so on. . .

We all, being spirit, soul and body, have to reach the end of our life-time.

o If we have **rejected** the Gift of God – Jesus and eternal life – then our unregenerated spirit and our *brute beast* or *life* or *body & soul* are consigned to hell.

o If we have **accepted** the Gift of God and become Born-Again, our *brute beast* or *life* or *body & soul* are regenerated by our living spirit and given eternal life, then we – body, soul and spirit are consigned to heaven.

Rejecting the Holy Spirit [in the form of the Spirit of Jesus] and despising His work (which is providing our salvation – among other things) is known as the *unforgivable sin*. But accepting Him and all He is, is salvation and the opportunity to enter into the Lord's covenants. As the Holy Spirit [in the form of the Spirit of Jesus], which is the very Life of God, enters our spirit, we, our spirits, are given His life.

Here is where we find the *two* or separation of the Believer and the unbeliever. Our paths diverge drastically from each other [2 Corinthians 6:15 *And what concord hath Christ with Belial? or what part hath he that believeth with an infidel?*].

With plants, we see that the *sperm* is the seed and the *egg* is the earth. As the seed penetrates the earth, the plant begins to grow. All animal and human life begins with the fusing of sperm and egg, which gives a body and a soul.

What separates man and animal is that God endows man with a spirit at conception[76]. It is for this reason that I refer to the body and soul as the *brute beast*. Unregenerated man can act like an animal because he is acting upon his instinct and not allowing his spirit the opportunity to guide him into a relationship with the life-giver – The Lord.

The condition of man before the flood was that fallen angels [devils] had mingled [had sex with] with human women and produced *brute beasts* without human spirits (as I explained elsewhere – they are called *nephilim*). This brought the judgement of God upon the world in the form of the Flood. We are facing another such judgement because we are seeing a resurgence of nephilim as well as the engineering of *human* life being *created* by man[77], thus creating other forms of *brute beast*. I am referring to genetic engineering as well as so-called *transcendent machines*.

These are *test-tube babies* combined with computer interfaces creating a human-machine or a machine-human. Why am I going here?

The end times shall be like the *time of Noah*. (Luke 17:26, 27. *26 And as it was in the days of Noe, so shall it be also in the days of the Son of man. 27 They did eat, they drank, they married wives, they were given in marriage, until the day that Noe entered into the ark, and the flood came, and destroyed them all.*) Just because our sin is more sophisticated than in the days of Noah, does not mean that it is not as evil or will not be judged.

The term *married wives* in this Scripture has the connotation of forcing the woman to be their wife. And the term *giving in marriage* carries with it the suggestion of all sexual perversion known to man and maybe even unknown to man. It means in essence that the act of sexual intercourse was performed consensually as well as without consent; with any partner, creature or object. The degradation was total (depth) and complete (quantitative).

If the enemy had succeeded in *defiling* all of mankind, then the Messiah would not have been able to be born of a virgin, as required by prophecy. Today, if the enemy can *defile* all of mankind, the Messiah would have no pure body for whom to return.

Today's degradation is termed "cloning" and "transcendent machines". In other words, man is genetically altering man and his DNA (in the way the satan desired to do before the flood).

Man WANTS God to be Just

I have had situations where (as an example) an unregenerated mind wanted to argue with me that God would/should take everyone to heaven. "After all, God is supposed to be a God of love!" they said "Why would he not want EVERYONE to go to heaven?" There is a Scripture that tells us that it is not the will of God that ONE should perish, but that ALL should be saved. We find this in 2 Peter 3:9 (*The Lord is not slack concerning his promise, as some men count slackness; but is longsuffering to us-ward, not willing that any should perish, but that all should come to repentance.*).

But this does not mean that all shall accept the sacrifice of Jesus and be saved! It just means that this is the desire of the Lord. Man still has his own will and is free to make his own decisions.

My reply (among other considerations) to such a person is found in the form of a few questions.

- ❖ Does that mean that the satan must come and live next to you in heaven?
- ❖ And what about Hitler that murdered 6 million Jews – just because they were Jews – and that is besides the murdering of the millions of his own people and others that were born with brown eyes or hair, or as a midget, or other 'deformities'?
- ❖ Or would you like mass murderers, paedophiles?
- ❖ Or how about those that machine-gunned school children at their school?
- ❖ Do you really want that person to live forever next-door to you in heaven?

Their, normally horrified, reply is a resounding 'NO!'

"So which evil sinner do **you** want living next door to you?"

After a few seconds thought the rather timid reply comes: -

"No! I guess I really do want God to be just."

The understanding that if God is lenient with one type of sin, He must be lenient with all types of sin, is not a concept that is hard to grasp. Only those that are Blood-Washed shall see the Kingdom of God and ultimately, Heaven.

Resurrection from the Dead and Eternal Judgement

Putting these together, we see Jesus being perfected in us and us working for God with the right attitude. This gives us assurance that we will never go to hell. That, is true ***Hope***.

We also see that God is a just judge and will require an answer from every person, for every action and even every idle word spoken, in his or her life. Only those whose lives are covered by, and influenced by, the blood and life of Jesus will face it confidently.

(John 5:30 I can of mine own self do nothing: as I hear, I judge: and my judgment is just; because I seek not mine own will, but the will of the Father which has sent me. Matthew 12:36 But I say unto you, That every idle word that men shall speak, they shall give account thereof in the day of judgment.)

I know there will be Confusion Concerning Eternal Judgement

The reason for this is mainly because the *end times* is a *seldom preached on* subject in these last days. But the Word says we should encourage one another with these words[78]. I shall now attempt to squeeze a summary of a subject that has been expounded in many a book, into a few lines or pages.

The first thing that needs to be understood is that the earth was **CREATED** by God about 6, 000 years ago. Do not allow yourself to be fooled by the *evolutionist's* lies. A "proof" of the fact of creation lies in the truth that God's perfect number is "7" on the one hand. And symbolically, "1, 000" speaks of a multitude

241

or many, on the other hand. With there being still 1,000 years of Jesus' ruling on the earth, personally, still to come, {which is known as the "millennium"}; it would make the time existing on the earth (as we know it) 7,000 years.

I am going to present a 'timeline' that will, hopefully, explain the entire history of the world in brief. I shall attempt to make it to scale.

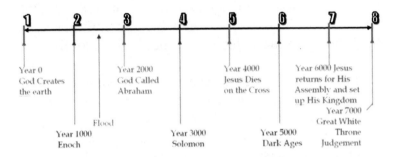

1) [Adam] God creates the heavens & the earth in six days and rests on the seventh day.

2) [Enoch] Enoch is born. He is symbolic of the Congregation being raptured before God's judgement, which was, in his case, the flood. The Congregation will be raptured before God judges the world in the *Tribulation*. (*Genesis 5:24 And Enoch walked with God: and he was not; for God took him; Hebrews 11:5 By faith Enoch was translated that he should not see death; and was not found, because God had translated him: for before his translation he had this testimony, that he pleased God.*)

3) [Abraham] God calls Abraham (the Father of Faith – who sacrificed Isaac in shadow) to leave

his land and go to a land that God would show him – and he went *not knowing*.

4) [Solomon] Solomon was another picture of Jesus, Who *shall build His Church.* (*Matthew 16:18 And I say also unto you, That you are Peter, and upon this rock I will build my church; and the gates of hell shall not prevail against it*).

5) [Servant Jesus] Jesus dies on the cross fulfilling over 1000 prophecies!

6) [Ishmael] The dark ages answers [in part] to the *great falling away* spoken of in 2 Thessalonians 2:3. (*2 Thessalonians 2:3 Let no man deceive you by any means: for that day shall not come, except there come a falling away first, and that man of sin be revealed, the son of perdition;*). This was the period when the Islamic religion influenced the world to a large extent. (The father of this group was Ishmael.)

7) [King Jesus] Just before Jesus sets up His Kingdom for 1000 years, which is to occur at this point, there is the *rapture of the Saints.* There are eight times more prophecies for the second coming of Jesus than there is for His first coming. Seeing that we KNOW that He came to die on the cross, we can know with equal certainty Jesus will come AGAIN! This period is preceded by the 3 ½ years of tribulation and 3 ½ years of **great** tribulation making up the "week" of *Jacob's trouble* spoken of in Jeremiah 30:7. (*Jeremiah 30:7 Alas! for that day is great, so that none is like it: it is even the time of Jacob's trouble; but he shall be saved out of it.*) This is when the satan is bound up for 1000 years (*Revelation 20:2 And he laid hold on the dragon, that old serpent, which is the Devil, and The satan, and bound him a thousand years,*) only to

be loosened *for a while* before the Great White Throne Judgment. Between the Rapture and the second coming, there should be a period of about 10 years. During this time there will be the judgment of the Saints at the **Throne of the Lamb** (*Revelation 7:9 After this I beheld, and, lo, a great multitude, which no man could number, of all nations, and kindreds, and people, and tongues, stood before the throne, and before the Lamb, clothed with white robes, and palms in their hands;*). Only after this judgment, can the Saints come with the Lord in *Great Glory*. Much more happens at this time, but let me leave this subject here.

8) [Judge Jesus] Here the unsaved, unregenerated and sinners are *translated*, raised and stand before the Great White Judgment Seat of God. (*Revelation 20:11 And I saw a great white throne, and him that sat on it, from whose face the earth and the heaven fled away; and there was found no place for them.*) Just before the Judgment seat appears, the satan is released to fool the nations into rebelling once again.

Chapter End Notes

74 Latin verb *Rapio*: To seize or to snatch away:
Rapture. The Hebrew understanding of the *Rapture*
is slightly different to the Western/Greek understanding. They view it as a *Harvesting*, and there
are four *Harvesting* events spoken of in Revelation.
I may deal with this a little more in my *Rabbit
Trails Book*.

75 We were indeed created in the image of God. Nose,
hands, and other such features, I can only suppose.
The fact of being a trinity (i.e. three in one; body
soul and spirit), which, in turn, is more critical to
understand. What I have said previously about
being created in the image of God and being a
trinity (three-in-one) still stands. What I am dealing
with here is the understanding of the *nuts and bolts*
of judgement. I link *natural man* and *spiritual man*
to their eternal habitations. To see the human spirit
(which comes from God) in the correct light is
important. The Holy Spirit, in the form of the *Spirit
of Jesus* – the seed or sperm {if I could parallel the
natural into the spiritual} – enters our spirit – the
egg {if I could parallel the natural into the spiritual}
and starts our eternal life which in turn regenerates
our soul – by the process of educating it in the
study of the Word and time spent in the presence
of the Lord – and shall (in the future) regenerate
our bodies.

76 Legal entrance to the earth (as a living being) is that
of a normal birth as we perceive it. Illegal entry is
by the creation of life without the *permission* of the
Lord (by virtue of His provision of a spirit to the
conceived *brute beast*).

77 A life can be built (engineered) by man, but it cannot possess a spirit because that is given by God only. Those created by God (also through the natural process of a man and woman joining their seed and egg) are the only humans that can have a spirit.

78 Hebrews 10:25. 25 Not forsaking the assembling of ourselves together, as the manner of some [is]; but exhorting [one another]: and so much the more, as ye see the day approaching.

Chapter 16

Maturing or Growing or Going on. . . .

Y ou will notice that this principle does not appear to have a partner. Nor does it get mentioned clearly in the list of principles. It <u>does</u> have a partner though; in fact, it has six partners. All the principles are to be affected by this principle. We never stop learning about God. Nor do we stop becoming more like Jesus! That is why it is mentioned as the first principle. I have made it the last one for emphasis.

> Luke 9:62. *62 And Jesus said to him, No man, having put his hand to the plough, and looking back, is fit for the kingdom of God.*

The parallel (about the athletes) that I have used in the "I Need You to Know" continues here. All the principles will be forever active in your life. The only difference is that they will be of a higher standard and requiring more faith and commitment. You can allow yourself to become *unfit* and *rusty*, as any athlete could;

but should one take their salvation and growth seriously, one would pass their experience on to the next *champion* by training them up in these same principles. In thus doing, causing the Kingdom of God to flourish and multiply.

In real terms, it means that you must take the responsibility for our own spiritual growth. You cannot expect your Brethren to "fetch and carry" you. More than that, it means that you must start to take responsibility of training someone else to: -

❖ Become a Christian
❖ Grow up in Christ
❖ Teach them all you know, and
❖ Teach them to do the same

Rabbit Trail Starts. . .

Looking at the Principles in a Symbolic form

Here is an explanation of some Biblical names.
Names: -

❖ Abraham – Father of a great multitude
❖ Isaac – Laughter
❖ Jacob – Heel-grabber (He will not allow the enemy to get away with anything)
❖ Israel – Soldier of God
❖ Jews – An Israelite (from Judah, meaning *praise*)
❖ Judah – Praise
❖ Gentile – Not a Jew

Why I would look at symbolism at all, is simply that God is *big on* symbolism. Much of prophecy, much of Scripture, many words of knowledge, words of wisdom, etc., are all shared in symbolic form. God takes His symbolism, and types, very seriously.

Moses was forbidden entry into the Promised Land because he struck the rock for water to come out (as he had done previously), instead of speaking to it as God had told him to do.

Exodus 17:6 *Behold, I will stand before you there upon the rock in Horeb; and you shall smite the rock, and there shall come water out of it, that the people may drink. And Moses did so in the sight of the elders of Israel.*

Here God had told Moses to strike the rock.

Numbers 20:8. *Take the rod, and gather you the assembly together, you, and Aaron your brother, and you speak unto the rock before their eyes; and it shall give forth his water, and you shall bring forth to them water out of the rock: so you shall give the congregation and their beasts drink.)*

Here, the second time, God told Moses to <u>speak</u> to the rock.

Exodus 20:11 *And Moses lifted up his hand, and with his rod he smote the rock twice: and the water came out abundantly, and the congregation drank, and their beasts [also].*

Instead of speaking to the rock, Moses <u>struck the rock in anger</u>.

Numbers 27:12 – 14. *12 And the LORD said unto Moses, Get you up into this mount Abarim, and see the land which I have given unto the children of Israel. 13 And when you have seen it, you also shall be gathered unto your people, as Aaron your brother was gathered. 14 For you rebelled against my commandment in the desert of Zin, in the strife of the congregation, to sanctify me at the water before their eyes: that [is] the water of Meribah in Kadesh in the wilderness of Zin.*

Because Moses had struck the rock instead of speaking to it, God forbade him entry into the Promised Land.

One may ask why the difference? The rock spoke of Jesus, who was first smitten (in death upon the cross) but after He is risen from the dead, there is no more condemnation for those in Christ Jesus. Jesus does not have to die a second time. Now God only has to speak to those in Jesus, to obtain obedience, and He does not have to judge them because Jesus was judged for us on the cross.

From Genesis, right down to the Book of the Revelation, God uses symbolism. When we try to understand the person of God, we use symbolism. When the future of the devil and his angels (demons or evil spirits) is described, symbolism is used.

Why?

Because we will find that the mind of a man can more easily grasp a meaning, or understand an intention [as an example]; that may be difficult to explain, by using symbolism and pictures. There is a saying in the world that runs like this: "A picture paints a thousand words." And this is true.

Should I explain the formation of a cloud, I could speak until the cloud had blown away and not succeed in expressing its beauty. But, let me show you a picture and the beauty will be apparent without me saying a word.

Some Biblical practices require symbolic accuracy, two of these are: -

❖ Baptism in Water.
❖ Breaking of Bread.

When it comes to water Baptism, infant baptism is an insult to the Lord. Water Baptism has been dealt with elsewhere in this book. You should therefore understand its importance already. When it comes to *christening*, this is a personal preference, but it cannot be called "Scriptural" or "Baptism". If a ship, for example, was *christened*, it would be given a name; should it be *baptized*, it would lie at the bottom of the sea - sunk.

Similarly, using bread with yeast, and wine with alcohol content, in the Breaking of Bread is also an insult to the Lord. The breaking of Bread symbolism is speaking of the Body and Blood of Jesus. Yeast and alcohol are both symbols of sin. There is no sin in Jesus and Jesus can never have sin. When Jesus died upon the cross He did not become a sinner, He became sin itself; and that, only for the purpose of burying our sin from the sight of God.

There are other symbolisms that are in Scripture that requires being accurate, but I do not intend dealing with all symbolism in this work.

If we then take the "Star of David[79]", we can see the foundation principles embodied in it.

The three *faith* ancestors become the representatives of God's promises, as well as the fulfilment of those promises, that we have seen in this study. Further, the representations of the three groupings, [i.e. the salvation, faith, and hope groups, as mentioned at the beginning of this book], are clearly seen.

(1) Star points 1 & 2; we see Abraham, the 'Friend of God' and the 'Father of Faith' represents the Salvation (or 'Love') Principles.

(2) Star points 3 & 4; we see the son of promise (with miraculous birth, who was sacrificed in type[80]), Isaac, represents the Faith Principles.

(3) Star points 5 & 6; we see the one that *formed* the "*Hebrew family*" Jacob, representing the Hope Principles. (He also had a miracle birth, and was the one who was favoured by God; and was out of the traditional *birth-line*, of inheritance.[81] As God had made promises to both Abraham and

Isaac, so Jacob was personally given promises as well. He was initially the despised one [by man] but became the fulfilment of the promises.)

We can also see the three patriarchs each repre-senting one of the personalities of the Godhead[82].

(1) Abraham represents God the Father.
(2) Isaac represents God the Son – Jesus.
(3) Jacob, renamed "Israel" represents God the Holy Spirit.

The parallel between the personalities of the Godhead and the patriarchs are quite striking. The parallel between Abraham and God the Father is quite easy to perceive. God is the Father that created the world by a word of faith. Abraham is the *father of faith* (those that believe God by faith and become God's child, are following the example of *father* Abraham, who "believed God and it was accounted to him for righteousness" - Galatians 3:6.

Isaac and Jesus are also easy enough to perceive, if you read the story of Isaac.

✓ Jesus was born of a virgin – a natural impossibility
✓ Isaac was born of a woman who was barren – a natural impossibility
✓ Jesus and Isaac were the special sons of their respective Fathers (Genesis 22:2. *And he said, Take now your son, your only [son] Isaac, whom you love, and you get into the land of Moriah; and offer him there for a burnt offering upon one of the mountains which I will tell you of.*)

- ✓ And Isaac was a shadow of the coming Messiah, Jesus.
- ✓ Also, Abraham was prepared to sacrifice his only son, his son of promise, Isaac, when Isaac was about 33 years old; as God did with Jesus, His only begotten Son, whom He loved, when Jesus was 33 years old.

The Holy Spirit, however, requires a bit more thought. The Holy Spirit is despised; strangely enough, by the very people that claim to be *Children of God*. The unbelievers and pagans also claim to know the Holy Spirit in their own brand of religion. God says that He shall not hold those guiltless who "take the Name of the Lord in vain" (Exodus 20:7).

This does not just imply using the Lord's Name as a swear-word (even though this is applicable) but it also means claiming to represent the Lord when you are actually His enemy. This behaviour is also known as "despising the Name of the Lord."

The word "despising" means, among other things, that you treat it as a common thing or misunderstand the importance of that particular thing (misrepresenting Him). Even treat it casually! This is how the Holy Spirit is being treated today, and this is how Jacob was treated by family and friends. But God saw him differently. God saw Jacob as a *prince with God*, which is what *Israel* means.

So we see that the Father, Son and Holy Ghost are represented in Abraham, Isaac and Jacob. In so many places in the Bible, we find the words ". . .the God of Abraham, Isaac and Jacob (or Israel). . ." and we just think of the fact that the Lord is their God. Now, I hope you can see another, deeper, implication. When one understands the practice and principles of the *blood covenant,* one would see how the giving of names applies here as well.

Another symbolic picture I would like to mention is that of a fruit tree (as the fig tree is used in the Bible to refer to Israel as a nation). But here I would like to use it simply to illustrate the Jewish/Gentile and Jewish/ Congregation relationship in a, sort-of, *big picture* over all the ages that the earth has been home to the human race.

The following chart and picture could give you an idea of the relationship of the principles as it involves the whole world through all of time: -

Linked Principles	Tree / Part	Nation
1) Repentance from dead works 2) Faith toward God (Salvation)	Root	Jews
3) Doctrine of Baptisms 4) Laying on of hands (Faith)	Trunk	Gentiles Inclu-ded/ Added
5) Resurrection from the Dead 6) Eternal Judgement (Hope)	Leaves and/or Fruit	The Congre-gation (Consis-ting of Jews & Gentiles)

Finally, our Heavenly Father initiated the reconciliation of man to Himself because He loved us so much. The only 'offspring' that He had was the miraculously born Jesus. Born of a virgin, born with no human father, and no-one knew where He *came from*. Israel began the family that became a mighty nation and a nation that despite concerted efforts by their many enemies, have risen from the dead (symbolically and literally). Yet, they have never ceased to exist as a peculiar *people of God*, even while scattered throughout the earth (as the Congregation is today).

When it comes to symbolism, typology and anti-types, the animal kingdom is often used. Here are some samples of animal parallels: -

(a) Pigs – Human beings. They eat any food placed before them – good or bad, spiritual or physical. Pigs cannot freely and willingly lift their heads to the heavens (it is a physical impossibility) – the human's sin prevents them seeking their Maker. Both, the pig and man, need help to achieve their objective. The pig speaks of the unregenerated man, rebellious and stiff-necked, which makes the man *unclean*.

(b) Sheep – Human beings. The sheep is totally harmless and defenceless. They are regarded as foolish because they seldom think for themselves, thus the saying: - "follow like sheep." They literally walk one-foot-in-front-of-the-other to the extent that sheep paths are about 2″ – 2 ½″ wide. They would need someone to look after them as they are incapable of looking after themselves. Even the smallest predator could prey on them. The human being cannot save himself and needs a Saviour. God desires to be our shepherd and has created us without natural defensive weapons. The sheep speak of regenerated man, harmless and defenceless and has recognized their need of a Saviour, which makes the man *clean*.

(c) Eagles – Believers. As eagles use the wind to rise up to "impossible" heights, so the Believer uses the Holy Spirit to rise to "impossible" heights. The eagle feasts on the enemy (snakes, rats, rabbits, etc.) and the Believer takes on their spiritual enemies just as easily.

(d) Doves – Believers (as well as the Holy Spirit). The dove has no glands that can absorb *poisons* in their bodies and therefore is regarded as a pure animal. The Believer is spiritually pure by the Holy Spirit.

(e) Bats – demons/evil spirits. These animals are nocturnal and are unclean. Some regard them as *creepy*. Many stories are spun about their blood-lust and attacks upon people. These stories are untrue as they seldom, if ever, prey upon humans in any way or form. God originally put a *fear* upon animals when it comes to man (but this has changed increasingly as sin rages unchecked upon the earth). No demon can touch a human without being invited to do so. evil spirits/devils are classed as unclean, stemming from their fall from heaven, in the rebellion when they followed the satans.

(f) Snakes – devils/evil spirits & the satan. From the Garden of Eden, when the satan tempted Eve. The snake is distrusted and is venomous and dangerous. Even harmless snakes are enemies of man. The curse upon the serpent holds true for the snake. The name *snake* and the name *serpent* are often used interchangeably. I suspect that the name *serpent* carries with it an inferred and added meaning. This meaning would be inherently evil, if my suspicions are correct. Either way, the symbolism is obvious, I think.

257

The only challenge with symbolism is to know when it is symbolic and when it is literal. The 'rule of thumb' to be used is that the symbolism is obvious from the context. If it is not obviously a symbolistic reference, it would be intended to be taken literally.

Rabbit Trail Ends. . .

Chapter End Notes

79 I do understand that the God-given symbol for Israel is the **Menorah**, but because the Israelis have chosen this *Star of David*, I have used it as it fits in very nicely indeed (in helping us understand and remember these principles).

80 *Type* means that this person was a picture of what was to come. It could be an object that is the picture of something yet to come. e.g. The blood of the sacrificial lambs were all pictures of the blood of Jesus yet to be shed. Or it could be a person that is the *type* for a person yet to come. e.g. Moses was a type of Jesus who was yet to come.

81 The eldest born was the one to receive the first and biggest inheritance, blessings, promises, etc. Esau [the older twin boy] lost his inheritance and his blessing to Jacob [the younger twin boy].

82 Godhead means *the Trinity* in the form of one co-equal, co-existent, co-powerful, co-creating, etc., single God, *Elohim* or as man calls Him - *Jehovah*.

Chapter 17

Good Advice

Read your Bible, Pray Everyday and find a Sound Church[83] to go to. . .

When you first accepted Jesus as Lord and Saviour, you were given some sound advice. You are inevitably told to "Read your Bible, Pray Everyday and find a Sound Church to go to. . ." This immediately raises questions like: -

- ✓ Where do I start reading the Bible?
- ✓ What is *Pray*?
- ✓ How do I pray?
- ✓ When do I pray?
- ✓ What is a *sound church*?
- ✓ How do I find one?
- ✓ Where do I find one?

Although this may be good advice, it is not always helpful. Giving helpful advice, on the other hand, is awkward. The reason for this is that it depends on where you are and the circumstances you face. No-one can give you perfect advice without knowing all the facts. Therefore, the advice I would like to impart to you would be broad and unspecific and not too helpful. I just hope it gives you enough to steer you in the right direction.

Firstly, Reading your Bible.

There are three criteria that you need to consider.

1. Your previous spiritual experience (were/are you a regular *church-goer*, a *backslider* or possibly an ex-heathen?)
2. Your available time (this may seem a silly thing, but often we set a regime for reading our new *best loved* book and when we fail to keep it up, we get discouraged and give it up altogether. Whereas if we set a realistic goal, we could keep it up indefinitely.)
3. Your commitment (a commitment, as in the *repentance* study, has to be a quality commitment with no plans to turn back. It also needs to be a sacrifice to the Lord.) [You may have to set an early 5:00am {with all things being equal} meeting time with your Heavenly Daddy. Religiously, this could be called a *quiet time*. I prefer to call it a *date with Daddy* or *My Time*. Call it nothing if you so desire, just spend it with your Bible.]
   a) If you already have a background of knowing the Scriptures, you could consider starting the New Testament with the idea of reading it through completely in six months and then start a new regime of reading the entire Bible in one year [book by book].

b) If you have never read the Bible before, read the first two books of the Bible first, then go on to the same advice in a) above.

c) Once you have read the entire Bible through, at least once, start over in reading the entire Bible [book by book] and spend time understanding or researching each verse – take your time!

With the Greek Mindset (as I mentioned in my comments about the Bible in chapter 1) we would see a Scripture and decide that it means *one* OR the *other* thing, but not both! (An example will be the infamous argument about the choice between "Law" and "Grace." It is seen as either: - We serve God by obeying His *Law* or we serve Him by *Grace* alone.)

Actually, Scripture operates on four levels simultaneously (according to the Hebrew language and understanding): -

(1) *pshof-* direct, simple; [Greek mindset style – sort of]
(2) *remez-* hinting;
(3) *darash* - commentary, comparison;
(4) *sod* - deep, hidden [needing further investigation].

Two examples I would like to use: -

1   Joshua 1:3 (*Every place that the sole of your foot shall tread upon, that have I given unto you, as I said to Moses.*)

a. (*pshof*) The simple or direct meaning: - In the new land that the Hebrews were about to enter, all the land would be theirs, that is, every place their foot stepped.

b. *(remez)* The hint: - They would have to actually walk on it to claim it.
c. *(darash)* The commentary or comparison: - They were previously slaves and could only go where they were permitted to by the Egyptians. Now they would be free to *go* and *be* what they desired.
d. *(sod)* The deep or hidden: - Any Believer has the victory over the *Egyptian* [the world system or situation] and has no need to fear any person [known as the "fear of man"] they are free to obey the Lord at every turn (even if they are in some sort of physical prison).
e. General comment: - This is a quick rendering just to illustrate my point and even further investigation is left up to you to embark upon.

2 Joshua 1:4 (*There shall not be any man able to stand before you all the days of your life: as I was with Moses, so I will be with you: I will not fail you, nor forsake you.*)

a. *(pshof)* The simple or direct meaning: - God was with Moses, and it was obviously so, by the miracles, signs and wonders that Moses displayed; and also the supernatural authority that he displayed before man. And, in the same way, God would be with Joshua.
b. *(remez)* The hint: - Joshua had to believe God's word as fact and walk in this knowledge [behave as Moses did].
c. *(darash)* The commentary or comparison: - Moses took on Pharaoh and the armies of Egypt and Joshua had to take on all the armies of all the land they were about to enter. He may have needed a greater anointing than

Moses had, because there were more armies
to be taken on than just the Egyptians – as
was the case with Moses.

d. (*sod*) The deep or hidden: - Any Believer can
walk with the knowledge and assurance that
the Lord is on his side and more than that,
He is with him wherever he may go. (This
is a deterrent for me to enter "unsavoury
places", because I refuse to take my Lord
into places like that, without good reason.)

e. General comment: - Again, this is a quick
rendering just to illustrate my point and
even further investigation is left up to you to
embark upon.

A parting shot.

We need to allow the Word of God to sink into our
hearts from our minds (more than just *soul knowledge*).
This is often the longest 18 inch journey on earth. To
illustrate my meaning, look at Joshua 1:6, 7 and 18.

> Joshua 1:6, 7 (6 *Be strong and of a good courage: for
> unto this people shall you divide for an inheritance
> the land, which I swear to their fathers to give them.
> 7 Only you be strong and very courageous, that you
> may observe to do according to all the Torah, which
> Moses my servant commanded you: turn not from it
> to the right hand or to the left, that you may prosper
> wheresoever you go.*)

Here God is encouraging Joshua to "be strong and
of good courage," twice! Then, the people following
Joshua, who had heard the encouragement and had

allowed the encouragement to "sink in" states to Joshua in verse 18: -

> Joshua 1:18 (*Whosoever he be that does rebel against your commandment, and will not hearken to your words in all that you command him, he shall be put to death:* **only be strong and of a good courage.**) [Emphasis mine.]

We need the Words of God to sink in and become *common* knowledge to us, so that others see us acting what we believe.

Secondly, Pray.

What does it mean to "Pray"?

➤ When you talk with your wife or husband, boss or servant, friend or legal representative, then you are having a *conversation*

➤ When you reprimand a child, chide an enemy or disagree with your wife (and sometimes your husband[84]), it is said that *you are fighting*

➤ When you speak to a devil or evil spirit, you are *rebuking*

➤ And so on. . .

➤ When you speak to God, however, this is called *Pray* or *Prayer*. It just means "speak with God". I say 'with' because it is a two-way conversation. God may or may not speak audibly, but He most certainly is not *silent*.

There are many *formulae* for the question "How do I pray."

⚓ One person tells you to start with, and finish with, praise.

⚓ Another says that you need to pray for an hour and follow the pattern of praise, ask for yourself, ask for others, ask for the Church and finish with thanks.

⚓ Yet others say that whatever you pray for; don't pray for yourself – that is prideful!

I think that you need to avoid following other's *systems* and spend time "Talking with Daddy". Yes, our God deserves Thanksgiving, Praise and Worship continually, but He knows there are issues that need attention too!

✓ Being benevolent in praying for others is a sign of your love for them.

✓ And, it is indeed necessary to pray for yourself, as you cannot be a blessing unless you are blessed (so ask God to bless you!).

✓ When you discuss things with **your earthly father** do you follow a regimented pattern?

✓ Or are there things you need to memorize, when talking to **your earthly father,** "in case" you anger him?

In South Africa, at a Rhema Conference one year a preacher, Ray Bevan from Wales, England, told us of an incident. He was preparing a message in his study and noticed the ice cream van passing by. His young son barged into his study and asked for an ice cream. As his son passed the window licking the ice cream a few minutes later, he sat back and revelled in the joy that the giving of that small gift had given him.

A *still small voice* spoke to his spirit: -
"Don't you think I would like to feel like that?"
Confused, he asked the Lord to explain.
"I too am a Father and I too enjoy giving My children gifts – both big and small!"
Ray realized that God's relationship to us is not "airy-fairy" or difficult to grasp or enjoy.[85]
If you were the child of the president of the largest/most powerful/wealthiest or whatever, country or company and again, or "whatever," you would be able to walk past the queue of patiently waiting ambassadors or representatives or officials and walk into your father's office – without an appointment – and discuss your problem or need with him. You take priority! Why? You are his special child. Maybe we do not have a father like that, but we are the children of the **Only Living God of Creation**! AND, He is NEVER too busy to see us!
So, how do you pray?

- ❖ Speak to your Daddy about what's on your heart and listen to what He has to say.
- ❖ The most important thing about prayer is not to be time-conscious or try spending 5 hours praying.
- ❖ Rather, be relationship conscious!
- ❖ Reading your Bible during prayer may very well give you a cause to pray as well[86].

As to **when** do you pray?

1 You can pray and. . .
2 You can pray *without ceasing.*
3 You can pray when you need to. . .

What I mean by 'pray and. . .' is that you can pray and *drive*, or pray and *iron*, or pray and *work on the car*, or pray and *wash dishes*, etc. God is interested in everything you do – big and small. Praying while doing something else simultaneously makes you conscious of His presence and involvement in your life at all times.

What I mean by *praying without ceasing* is; realizing the dynamic presence of the Lord with you at all times (Joshua 1:9). Realize that everything you say is spoken to the Lord as well as to whomever you are speaking at the time. [Hebrews 13:5 *Let your conversation be without covetousness; and be content with such things as you have: for he has said, I will never leave thee, nor forsake thee.*] If you say or do something good, you can immediately speak to the Lord and thank Him for His wisdom or ability to have done such a good thing (not necessarily praying aloud). And, if you do not know what to do next, you can ask Him immediately, and He shall give you the answer.

Then, of course, there are the times when a specific topic needs to be broached. You set aside a time and get on with discussing it with your loving Father. There is not a time on the face of the earth that you cannot speak to your Father.

You shall find in your travels that the Preachers will often use an example of when you pray, ". . .Even if God awakes you at 3 o' clock in the morning. . ." they will say. The truth of the matter is that medically, or scientifically, one is in their deepest sleep at 3 a.m. and this is when it is most difficult to arouse a sleeper. Should you wake up at 3 a.m. for no apparent reason, take it from me, God is calling you to prayer!

This is indeed a time that the Lord seems to choose to call His Saints and Watchmen to fill the gap for some reason. Also, He seems to be looking for people, at that time of the day, to speak to and give visions, words, etc.

Respond to the Lord in prayer, get up, dress warmly (if appropriate) and go to your *prayer closet*[87] and ask God what is on **His** heart. Listen and then pray it through! You shall <u>know</u> when you are finished praying. [God makes your short sleep sufficient for the next day if you trust Him and obey His call to prayer.]

One day, I tried to do as David did in the Psalms. David would ask God to kill his enemies; he called curses upon his enemies, breathing vengeance, and did all sorts of other soul-baring things. I began similarly "throwing my toys out of my cot" with the Lord, as I saw David had done. The Lord's rebuke was swift and certain! He made it VERY PLAIN to me that I was **not** David and I should **not** try to "wear his armour". I have since realized that I am my own individual; don't try to be someone else!

Thirdly, Find a 'Sound Church' to attend.

I know of no *Church* that operates as the Congregations did in the time of Paul and the other Apostles. I have heard people claim that *their* Church operated as in the time of the Apostles. I therefore visited some of them and I was disappointed to find the "same old, same old". The reason I say this is that you should not expect to find a perfect Congregation. What I'm saying is that a *Sound Church* is not easy to find. Ask questions, and do ask for a *statement of belief* from a leader or helper in the Congregation. They would gladly give you one, if they don't, "keep on trucking!"

But this is still not a *failsafe*. Certain Traditional Churches I've visited, for example, state that they believe in the Holy Spirit in their *statement of faith*; but then they teach that "the only, and all," the Holy Spirit you "will ever receive," is the Holy Spirit you receive at your salvation. Oops! No way! Yet on many other doctrines, they are sound.

Most, if not all, traditional Churches have camped[88] with the particular teaching that they hold dear. With this *camping* they have slowly been accepting error and diluting the message they preach. Examples of obvious error that they have accepted are: - evolution, political correctness, debates on moral issues and being *community conscious*[89].

You would have to attend for an appreciable period of time without becoming too *involved*. In this time you would find out whether the principles spoken of in this book are practiced and to what extent. Most times, a Congregation that is moving with God and becomes the focus of criticism, is normally a *Sound Church*. The *camped* or *traditional* "Church" is normally the first to condemn Assemblies that are following with the latest "move" of God. The *latest move* today is "Going back to our Jewish roots", and by extension, intimacy with the Lord. The newest name is "Messianic Judaism" and they meet in what they (correctly) call a "Messianic Jewish Synagogue."

How and **Where** you will find one is dependent upon where you are. Sorry, that is up to you to investigate and find the best Congregation for you. All I can say at this point is that a *Sound Church* would normally be an *independent Church*. (Not one of the well-known or *main-line Churches*.)

Chapter End Notes

83 The use of the word "Church" here is for the sake of simplicity of understanding.

84 Humour intended.

85 This is not a quote, but my own paraphrase.

86 This morning, as I read the Word and prayed, the Scripture spoke of God's punishment of His chosen people for disobedience. He was scattering them throughout the earth. I felt His pain at having to punish the *apple of His eye*, and I felt their pain in the suffering they endured (including the 6 million murdered by Hitler). I wept like a baby and cried to God. . ."Isn't it time for you to restore them Lord? Give them the peace that you promised the patriarchs.". . .And in this vein, I continued to pray. . .(I prayed for the pain of God, the pain of the Jews, for justice for the Jews, for judgement of the nations that are persecuting them, and for redemption and blessing for the Jews.) When I finished and dried my tears, I knew I was finished praying for the Jewish people; but there was just something that still needed to do to end off my prayer time. I spread myself on the floor in worship of my God. Only when I returned to bed, I realized that I had spent about two hours in prayer. I followed no "pattern", I just spent time in the presence of my King, my Lord, my Friend and my most precious Daddy.

87 Have a place or a chair that you can call *your place of contact* with the Lord. [Even if it is the toilet, if the toilet is the only place that you can spend time on your own.] It could be on a rock under a tree if you are honoured enough to have this option. A kitchen chair, a study chair – not the one you use for normal work or other such activity – a bench in

the garden, or wherever you chose to make your regular meeting place with the Lord.

88 *Camping, Camped, Camp*, or related references do not refer to the traditional idea of tents, campfires, and the singing of "Kumbaya". Rather it refers to their stopping of their walk with God at a particular teaching that, for them, is palatable. The correct attitude towards following the Lord should be one of ever growing and ever learning. Because they have chosen to stop, this does not mean they are rejected by God, it just means that He is disappointed to lose their commitment and fellowship.

89 The error to be found in being "community conscious" is that they attempt to superimpose the *community activity* that belongs to the Assembly of God's Children onto the community of pagan unbelievers. The *going into the market places* is to *preach the Gospel* not for charitable works or giving gifts. When the Congregation's needs are seen to, then you can consider blessing the unbelievers, but only as a means of evangelism – With **Fruit!**

Chapter 18

God's Word?

" I don't like the King James Version because it is so hard to understand!"

"I like the Message Bible, it is so easy to understand and it uses today's language!"

"The most popular Bible is the NIV. . ."

These, and many others, are comments that have been said to me and that I have heard said from time to time. One would imagine that the Bible is, surely, the Bible and it cannot change; or, *newer versions* only make it easier to understand, with our evolving languages.

All I can say is: - "I _**wish**_ that this was so!"

Imagine asking a child molester or paedophile to baby-sit your small children. Or perhaps, asking Hitler to write a book on: - "The preservation of the Jews."

In the same way, would you ask an infidel or a "satanist" to rewrite the Bible? Well, this is, in fact, a simile of what has happened with some versions of the Bible. Unbelievers and agnostics attempt to present a "more accurate" Bible and thereby purposely mislead with alternative word usage. (Like the inappropriate use of *Assyrian*, in the New International Version of the Bible, where it should read *Hebrew*.)

The *King James Version* does have some errors (like transliterating "baptism" instead of using the correct word "dip" or "submerge", and so on; as well as not being conducive (helpful) to understanding the Hebrew language). And, it has some difficult ancient English language to contend with.

But it is in fact the most **trustworthy** of the available Bibles around. That is if we do not take the Hebrew versions into account. I am speaking here of available English translations/paraphrases. Without going into *all* the bad points of the different versions, I have inserted a list of Scripture verses that you can compare to your current Bible.

But, I do need to explain some implications and give several examples, to make my point.

An Explanation

Using the "Message" as a comparison with the "King James": -

Illustration	KJV	The Message	Implication
The word "LORD" appears:	7900 times	71 times	Is God not LORD?
The words "Lord Jesus" appears:	118 times	0 times	Deity of Jesus neglected/denied?'
The words "Lord Jesus Christ" appears:	84 times	0 times	Deity of Jesus neglected/denied?

And again, using the "NIV" as a comparison with the "King James": -

The NIV has made 3600 important changes to the text of the Holy Bible that is expressly forbidden in Revelation 22:18, 19; Proverbs 30:5, 6; Galatians 3:10, 15[90].

The NIV has changed 2000 texts from singular to plural ('I' to 'us', etc.) thereby removing any personal responsibility to God for our personal actions and sins.

The NIV has changed 1600 references to sexual genders. Herewith, they claim (as an example) that God is female, and from what was previously explained, God calls Himself "Father".

The NIV has added the word "Pharisees" to the text of the Holy Bible where it does not apply, and that action is expressly forbidden in Revelation 22: 18, 19; Proverbs 30:5, 6; Galatians 3:10, 15.

The NIV has removed the word "Sadducees" from the text of the Holy Bible where it does apply, and that action is expressly forbidden in Revelation 22: 18, 19; Proverbs 30:5, 6; Galatians 3:10, 15.

What you need to look for is whether the verse contains the correct meaning and has not left out the pertinent or key thoughts or words.

Examples

As an example of the impact of changing Scripture: - The Scriptures mention that Jesus is the FIRST-BORN son of Miriam. Without this fact, it can remove the **miraculous virgin birth** of Jesus for the critic. Which in turn opens the door to speculation that Jesus could have been the son of Joseph or the result of some illegitimate relationship on Miriam's part. For Jesus to be a sinless substitutionary Lamb for us, He had to be the offspring of God the Father. Losing this fact erodes the young believer's faith.

A further example is that the Scriptures mention the Blood of Jesus being shed for our sins. The omission from Scripture of His Holy Blood removes the very thing, and the ONLY thing, that can eradicate our sins. In doing this, the door is opened, not only to the power of *sins forgiven* being lost, but it lowers our service to our God to *just another religion*.

Another disturbing example is that the Name of our Lord Jesus Christ is totally omitted from some translations as well as singular pronouns are changed to plural (like the Message). The upshot of this is (in the case of the omission of the Name of our Lord Jesus Christ) obviously to reduce our salvation experience to a system of powerless religious observances; and, (in the case of making singular into plural) to the removal of personal accountability before God.

Then, of course, you get the radically ill-advised versions that change our Heavenly Father into a woman. This is purely motivated by the promotion of being "Politically Correct" (correct translation: - "tool of the satan to hinder God's divine plan").

It *may* be difficult to *get your head around* the King James Version terminology. But, the poetical writing has been proven to be easy to memorize accurately. When it comes to accurately studying the Word of God, none can compare (English Versions). Do not get me wrong, I concede the difficult reading and unclear phraseology, and I do sympathize. I have succeeded in adapting my thinking and reading skill to read the 'thee's' and 'thou's', etc., as 'you' and 'your', etc., and I believe you can too – if you choose to do so. This assumes that you have not yet obtained an English Hebrew Bible (like the "Complete Jewish Bible"

Translated by David H. Stern). [I do not know if there is a concordance for it yet, but there is a commentary available for it.]

Following is but a sample of the Scriptures changed by unbelievers to belittle, discredit and adversely alter the Love Letter of our God to His People. You need to check your Bible against this list; and any other difference between them should be considered with this question: -

"Why. . .What is gained or lost by this difference?"

The following table (under "BIBLE Versions comparison list" – Below) lists 300 verses that have been changed in the seven most popular versions (New Testament Only).

Chapter End Notes

90 Revelations 22:18, 19. *18 For I testify unto every man that hears the words of the prophecy of this book, If any man shall add unto these things, God shall add unto him the plagues that are written in this book: 19 And if any man shall take away from the words of the book of this prophecy, God shall take away his part out of the book of life, and out of the holy city, and [from] the things which are written in this book.*

Proverbs 30:5, 6. *5 Every word of God [is] pure: he [is] a shield unto them that put their trust in him. 6 Add thou not unto his words, lest he reprove thee, and thou be found a liar.*

Galatians 3:10, 15. *10 For as many as are of the works of the law are under the curse: for it is written, Cursed [is] every one that continues not in all things which are written in the book of the law to do them. 15 Brethren, I speak after the manner of men; Though [it be] but a man's covenant, yet [if it be] confirmed, no man disannuls, or adds thereto.*

Conclusion

This study is designed for the sharing of these principles in the following forums: -

- This book could be handed out to the new-born Believer at the time of their Salvation and they can get on with being grounded and *followed-up* without the evangelist worrying about their future when he moves on
- For the *new-born* Believer to be grounded, by personal study
- For the Believer that is faced with the question "What do I believe?"
- For the Believer that is being hounded by false doctrine and needs to identify the true from the false
- For the concerned Believer that wants to ground other young Believers in the Word so that they will not *backslide*
- For the Believer that wants to practice his *teaching skills*
- For the person wanting the truth and has determined to earnestly seek it out

- For cell groups or Bible study groups that are starting out and seeking sound material for mutual edification.
- For the "surface scanner" and the "miner" alike (one can take it as a quick study, or one can research deeper to find more applications than is given here)

While installing these principles in your life, as a daily practice, you begin to mature and become strengthened in "the inner man". You begin to build your house upon the Rock and will not be moved.

False teaching becomes no threat at all. A practice that the banks have for training their people to spot counterfeit money is not to let them see and handle forgeries. Rather they let them only handle the real money. They get so used to the feel of the *real thing* that as soon as they handle a forgery, they <u>know</u> there is something wrong. They may not know what, but there is an alert in their feeling of the money.

So it is with these principles. As you get to know them more intimately, the better and quicker you will recognize a false teaching. You may not know what the error is, but your spirit will cry against it. You also need to trust that *feeling* because it is spirit-based.

I know of folk to whom I taught these principles, and they grew greatly in the spirit. In the course of our lives, we went our way and they went theirs. We *bumped* into them a few years later to find that they had not only grown in the Lord, but were active and valued members of the Congregation where they fellowshipped.

I believe in the *grounding* of these Basic Principles.

Prayer

Prince of Peace
by Akiane Kramarik

I pray that this study would be anointed in <u>your</u> hands to eat *the bread I have broken,* sharing it and growing, in the knowledge of Yeshuah Ha Mashiach, to the glory of God the Father, by the power of the Holy Spirit.

I pray that <u>you</u> would be motivated to recognize sin for what it is, repent of it, and get about growing spiritually.

May God bless <u>you</u>, and while He is blessing <u>you</u>, may He "bless <u>you</u> good!"

May God keep <u>you</u> from all evil and visit <u>you</u> with His presence constantly.

May God graciously cause <u>you</u> to expand your borders and raise You up into the ministry that He has called <u>you</u> to practice.

May <u>you</u> be a blessing, not a burden, to those around <u>you</u>.

May God bless <u>you</u> and keep <u>you</u> as <u>you</u> study and practise the Christian Walk.

With love from your Brother in Christ,

Ian.

The BEGINNING!

Recommended Reading and Bibliography

F urther reading to expand your understanding of some of the topics mentioned in this study follow: -

- ➤ Any of the excellent and priceless resources from **Answers in Genesis**
- ➤ Archaeology and Bible History by Joseph Free
- ➤ Complete Jewish Bible - translation by David H. Stern
- ➤ Cosmic Codes by Chuck Missler
- ➤ Dialogue with God by Mark Virkler
- ➤ Elements of Worship by Judson Cornwall
- ➤ FORBIDDEN GATES HOW GENETICS, ROBOTICS, ARTIFICIAL INTELLIGENCE, SYNTHETIC BIOLOGY, NANOTECH-NOLOGY, and HUMAN ENHANCEMENT HERALD THE DAWN OF TECHNODIMEN-SIGNAL SPIRITUAL WARFARE. By Thomas & Nita Horn
- ➤ God's War on Terror by Wallid Shoebat
- ➤ Israel and the Church by Ronald E. Diprose
- ➤ "It is often said" by Tim Hegg (Series)
- ➤ Kingdom of the Cults by Dr. Walter Martin
- ➤ Learn Biblical Hebrew by John H. Dobson

- Lost in Translation by John Klein & Adam Spears
- Numbers in Scripture by E.W. Bullinger
- Other books by Dr. Walter Martin
- Other books sold through FFOZ (First Fruits of Zion)
- Our Father Abraham by Marvin R. Wilson
- Pagan Christianity by Frank Viola and George Barna
- Praying the Scriptures by Judson Cornwall
- The Apostolic Ministry by Rick Joyner
- The Book of Enoch the Prophet by R.H. Charles
- The Everlasting Hatred the Roots of Jihad by Hal Lindsey
- The King James Bible with clarification modifications by Ian Foyn
- The Signature of God Grant R. Jeffrey
- The Spirit Himself by Ralph M. Riggs
- The teaching of Ron Saxby on the Basic Principles
- The Two Babylons by Rev Alexander Hislop
- Walking in the Dust of Rabbi Jesus by Lois Tverberg
- Yeshua by Dr. Ron Moseley

BIBLE Versions comparison list

THE SEVEN MOST POPULAR VERSIONS

NIV New International Version
NKJ New King James Version
NRS New Revised Standard Version
NC   New Century Version
NAS New American Standard Version
RSV Revised Standard Version
LB   The Living Bible
REM Has been Removed
CHG Has been Changed

VERSE	DESCRIPTION OF CHANGE	CHANGE IN...
Matthew 1:25	REM "Firstborn"	NIV, NAS, RSV, NRS, LB, NC
Matthew 5:22	REM "without a cause"	NIV, NAS, RSV, NRS, LB, NC
Matthew 5:44	REM 12 WORDS "bless them that curse you. . ."	NIV, NAS, RSV, NRS, LB, NC

Matthew 6:13	REM LAST 14 WORDS (For thine is the kingdom. . .)	NIV, NAS, RSV, NRS, LB, NC
Matthew 6:27	CHG "cubit to his stature" TO "hour to his life" et. al.	NIV, NAS, RSV, NRS, LB, NC
Matthew 6:33	REM "of God"	NIV, NAS, RSV, NRS, LB, NC
Matthew 8:29	REM "Jesus"	NIV, NAS, RSV, NRS, LB, NC
Matthew 9:13	REM "to repen-tance" (see also Mark 2:17)	NIV, NAS, RSV, NRS, LB, NC
Matthew 11:23	REM "hell"	NIV, NAS, NKJ, RSV, NRS, NC
Matthew 12:6	REM "one greater" TO "some-thing greater"	NAS, RSV, NRS, NC
Matthew 12:35	REM "of the heart"	NIV, NAS, RSV, NRS, NC
Matthew 12:40	CHG "whale" TO "fish", "sea monster"	NIV, NAS, NKJ, NRS, LB, NC
Matthew 12:47	REM ENTIRE VERSE	NIV, RSV, NRS,
Matthew 13:51	REM "Lord"	NIV, NAS, RSV, NRS, LB, NC
Matthew 15:8	REM "draweth nigh unto me with their mouth"	NIV, NAS, RSV, NRS, LB, NC
Matthew 16:3	REM "o ye hypocrites"	NIV, NAS, RSV, NRS, LB, NC
Matthew 16:18	REM "hell"	NIV, NAS, NKJ, RSV, NRS, NC
Matthew 16:20	REM "Jesus"	NIV, NAS, RSV, NRS, LB, NC

Matthew 17:21	REM ENTIRE VERSE	NIV, NAS, RSV, NRS, NC
Matthew 18:11	REM ENTIRE VERSE (key verse)	NIV, NAS, RSV, NRS, NC
Matthew 18:26	REM "and worshipped him" (for Jesus)	NIV, NAS, NKJ, RSV, NRS, NC
Matthew 19:9	REM LAST 11 WORDS	NIV, NAS, RSV, NRS, LB, NC
Matthew 19:17	CHG "Why callest thou me good" TO "Why do you ask me about what is good"	NIV, NAS, RSV, NRS, NC
Matthew 19:17	REM "God"	NIV, NAS, RSV, NRS
Matthew 20:7	REM "and what- soever is right that shall ye receive"	NIV, NAS, RSV, NRS, LB, NC
Matthew 20:16	REM "for many be called but few chosen"	NIV, NAS, RSV, NRS, LB, NC
Matthew 20:20	CHG "worship- ping him" TO "kneeling down"	NIV, NAS, RSV, NRS
Matthew 20:22	REM 12 WORDS "baptized with Christ's baptism"	NIV, NAS, RSV, NRS, LB, NC
Matthew 21:44	REM ENTIRE VERSE	NIV, RSV, NRS, NC
Matthew 23:14	REM ENTIRE VERSE	NIV, NAS, RSV, NRS, NC
Matthew 23:33	CHG "damnation" TO "con- demn", et. al.	NIV, NAS, NKJ, RSV, NRS, LB, NC
Matthew 24:36	ADD "nor the Son"	NIV, NAS, RSV, NRS, LB, NC

Matthew 24:36	CHG "my Father" TO "the Father"	NIV, NAS, RSV, NRS, LB, NC
Matthew 25:13	REM "wherein the Son of man cometh"	NIV, NAS, RSV, NRS, LB
Matthew 27:35	REM LAST 25 WORDS	NIV, NAS, RSV, NRS, LB, NC
Matthew 27:54	CHG "the Son of God" TO "a son of God"	NIV, NAS, RSV, NRS, LB, NC
Matthew 28:2	REM "from the door"	NIV, NAS, RSV, NRS, LB, NC
Matthew 28:9	REM "And as they went to tell his disciples"	NIV, NAS, RSV, NRS, LB, NC
Mark 1:1	REM "the Son of God"	NIV, NAS, RSV, NRS, NC
Mark 1:2	CHG "prophets" TO "Isaiah" (blatant LIE)	NIV, NAS, RSV, NRS, LB, NC
Mark 1:14	REM "of the kingdom" (gospel. . .of God)	NIV, NAS, RSV, NRS, LB, NC
Mark 1:31	REM "immediately"	NIV, NAS, RSV, NRS, LB, NC
Mark 2:17	REM "to repentance"	NIV, NAS, NKJ, RSV, NRS, NC
Mark 3:29	CHG "eternal damnation" TO "eternal sin", et al.	NIV, NAS, NKJ, RSV, NRS, LB, NC
Mark 6:11	REM LAST 23 WORDS	NIV, NAS, RSV, NRS, NC
Mark 7:8	REM LAST 15 WORDS	NIV, NAS, RSV, NRS, LB, NC
Mark 7:16	REM ENTIRE VERSE	NIV, NAS, RSV, NRS, LB, NC

Mark 9:24	REM "Lord" (refers to Jesus)	NIV, NAS, RSV, NRS, LB, NC
Mark 9:44	REM ENTIRE VERSE (about hell)	NIV, NAS, RSV, NRS, LB, NC
Mark 9:46	REM ENTIRE VERSE (about hell)	NIV, NAS, RSV, NRS, LB, NC
Mark 9:49	REM "and every sacrifice shall be salted with salt"	NIV, NAS, RSV, NRS, LB, NC
Mark 10:21	REM "take up the cross"	NIV, NAS, RSV, NRS, LB, NC
Mark 10:24	REM "for them that trust in riches"	NIV, NAS, RSV, NRS, NC
Mark 11:10	REM "that cometh in the name of the Lord"	NIV, NAS, RSV, NRS, LB, NC
Mark 11:26	REM ENTIRE VERSE	NIV, NAS, RSV, NRS, LB, NC
Mark 12:23	REM "when they shall rise"	NIV, RSV, NRS, LB,
Mark 12:40	CHG "greater damnation" TO "punished most severely", "greater condemnation"	NIV, NAS, NKJ, RSV, NRS, LB, NC
Mark 13:6	CHG "I am Christ" TO "I am He", "the One"	NIV, NAS, NKJ, RSV, NRS, LB, NC
Mark 13:14	REM "spoken of by Daniel the prophet"	NIV, NAS, RSV, NRS, LB, NC
Mark 13:33	REM "and pray"	NIV, NAS, RSV, NRS, LB, NC
Mark 14:68	REM "and the cock crew"	NIV, NAS, RS
Mark 15:28	REM ENTIRE VERSE	NIV, NAS, RSV, NRS, LB, NC

Mark 16:9-20	REM ENTIRE LAST 12 VERSES of Mark 16!	NIV, NAS, RSV, NRS, LB, NC
Luke 1:28	REM "blessed art thou among women"	NIV, NAS, RSV, NRS, LB, NC
Luke 2:14	CHG "good will toward men" TO "to men on whom his favour rests" et al	NIV, NAS, RSV, NRS, LB, NC
Luke 2:22	CHG "her" TO "their" (makes Jesus a sinner)	NIV, NAS, RSV, NRS, NC
Luke 2:33	CHG "Joseph" TO "his father" (attacks virgin birth)	NIV, NAS, RSV, NRS, NC
Luke 2:43	CHG "Joseph and his mother" TO "parents"	NIV, NAS, RSV, NRS, LB, NC
Luke 4:4	REM "but by every word of God"	NIV, NAS, RSV, NRS, LB, NC
Luke 4:8	REM "get thee behind me, The satan"	NIV, NAS, RSV, NRS, LB, NC
Luke 4:18	REM 8 WORDS "he hath sent me to heal. . ."	NIV, NAS, RSV, NRS, NC
Luke 4:41	REM "Christ"	NIV, NAS, RSV, NRS, LB, NC
Luke 6:48	CHG "founded upon a rock" TO "well built"	NIV, NAS, RSV, NRS, LB, NC
Luke 9:54	REM "even as Elijah did"	NIV, NAS, RSV, NRS, LB, NC
Luke 9:55	REM 9 WORDS "ye know not what manner of spirit. . ."	NIV, NAS, RSV, NRS, LB, NC

Luke 9:56	REM FIRST 16 WORDS For the Son of man is not come to destroy men's lives, but to save them."	NIV, NAS, RSV, NRS, LB, NC
Luke 9:57	REM "Lord"	NIV, NAS, RSV, NRS, LB, NC
Luke 10:15	REM "hell"	NIV, NAS, NKJ, RSV, NRS, NC
Luke 11:2	REM 15 WORDS from 'Lord's prayer'	NIV, NAS, RSV, NRS, LB, NC
Luke 11:4	REM "but deliver us from evil" (Lord's prayer)	NIV, NAS, RSV, NRS, LB, NC
Luke 11:29	REM "the prophet"	NIV, NAS, RSV, NRS, LB, NC
Luke 16:23	REM "hell"	NIV, NAS, RSV, NRS, LB, NC
Luke 17:36	REM ENTIRE VERSE	NIV, NAS, RSV, NRS, LB, NC
Luke 21:4	REM "cast in unto the offer-ings of God"	NIV, NAS, RSV, NRS, LB, NC
Luke 21:8	CHG "I am Christ" TO "I am He", "the One"	NIV, NAS, NKJ, RSV, NRS, LB, NC
Luke 22:64	REM "they struck him on the face"	NIV, NAS, RSV, NRS, NC
Luke 23:17	REM ENTIRE VERSE	NIV, NAS, RSV, NRS, LB, NC
Luke 23:38	REM "letters of Greek, Latin, Hebrew"	NIV, NAS, RSV, NRS, LB, NC
Luke 23:42	REM "Lord" (thief on the cross - get-ting saved!)	NIV, NAS, RSV, NRS, LB, NC

Luke 24:6	REM "He is not here, but is risen"	RSV, NRS
Luke 24:49	REM "of Jerusalem"	NIV, NAS, RSV, NRS, LB
John 1:14, 18	REM "begot-ten"(refers to Jesus)	NIV, NAS, RSV, NRS, LB, NC
John 1:27	REM "is preferred before me"	NIV, NAS, RSV, NRS, LB, NC
John 3:13	REM "which is in heaven" (refers to Jesus)	NIV, NAS, RSV, NRS, LB, NC
John 3:15	REM "should not perish" (believeth in him. . .)	NIV, NAS, RSV, NRS, LB, NC
John 3:16	REM "begotten"	NIV, NAS, RSV, NRS, LB, NC
John 3:18	REM "begotten"	NIV, NAS, RSV, NRS, LB, NC
John 4:24	CHG "God is a Spirit" TO "God is Spirit"	NIV, NAS, NKJ, RSV, NRS, LB, NC
John 4:42	REM "the Christ"	NIV, NAS, RSV, NRS, LB, NC
John 5:3	REM LAST 7 WORDS	NIV, NAS, RSV, NRS, LB, NC
John 5:4	REM ENTIRE VERSE	NIV, NAS, RSV, NRS, LB, NC
John 5:16	REM "and sought to slay him"	NIV, NAS, RSV, NRS, LB, NC
John 5:29	CHG "damnation" TO "condemn", "judgement"	NIV, NAS, NKJ, RSV, NRS, LB, NC
John 6:47	REM "on Me" (He that believeth. . .)	NIV, NAS, RSV, NRS, NC
John 6:69	CHG "Christ, the Son of the living God" TO "Holy One of God"	NIV, NAS, RSV, NRS, LB, NC

John 7:53-8:11	REM VERSES 7:53 - 8:11	NIV, NAS, RSV, NRS, LB, NC
John 8;9	REM "being convicted by their own conscience"	NIV, NAS, RSV, NRS, LB, NC
John 8:47	REM "heareth God's words" TO "hears what God says"	NIV, NC
John 8:59	REM LAST 10 WORDS "going through the midst. . ."	NIV, NAS, RSV, NRS, LB, NC
John 9:4	CHG "I must work the works" TO "We must work the works"	NIV, NAS, RSV, NRS, LB, NC
John 9:35	CHG "Son of God" TO "Son of Man", "Messiah"	NIV, NAS, RSV, NRS, LB, NC
John 11:41	REM "For the place where the dead was laid"	NIV, NAS, RSV, NRS, LB, NC
John 14:2	CHG "mansions" TO "rooms", "dwelling places"	NIV, NAS, NKJ, RSV, NRS, LB, NC
John 14:16	CHG "Comforter" TO "Helper", "Counsellor", et. al.	NIV, NAS, NKJ, RSV, NRS, NC
John 16:16	REM "because I go to the Father"	NIV, NAS, RSV, NRS, LB, NC
John 17:12	REM "in the world"	NIV, NAS, RSV, NRS, LB, NC
Acts 1:3	CHG "infallible" TO "con-vincing" et al.	NIV, NAS, RSV, NRS, LB, NC
Acts 2:30	REM "he would raise up Christ"	NIV, NAS, RSV, NRS, LB, NC

Acts 2:31	REM "hell"	NIV, NAS, NKJ, RSV, NRS, NC
Acts 2:38	CHG "remission of sins" TO "forgiveness of sins"	NIV, NAS, RSV, NRS, LB, NC
Acts 4:27,30	CHG "holy child" TO "holy servant" (attacks deity)	NIV, NAS, NKJ, RSV, NRS, LB, NC
Acts 7:30	REM "of the Lord" (angel of the Lord)	NIV, NAS, RSV, NRS, LB, NC
Acts 7:37	REM "Him shall ye hear"	NIV, NAS, RSV, NRS, LB, NC
Acts 8:37	REM ENTIRE VERSE (major salvation verse)	NIV, NAS, RSV, NRS, LB, NC
Acts 9:5	REM "it is hard for thee to kick against the pricks"	NIV, NAS, RSV, NRS, LB, NC
Acts 10:6	REM "he shall tell thee what thou oughtest to do"	NIV, NAS, RSV, NRS, LB, NC
Acts 15:11	REM "Christ"	NIV, NAS, RSV, NRS, LB, NC
Acts 15:18	CHG "beginning of the world" TO "...eternity", "...ages"	NIV, NAS, NKJ, RSV, NRS, LB, NC
Acts 15:34	REM ENTIRE VERSE	NIV, NAS, RSV, NRS, LB, NC
Acts 16:31	REM "Christ" (Believe on the Lord Jesus Christ)	NIV, NAS, RSV, NRS, LB, NC
Acts 17:16	CHG "stirred" TO "provoked", "distressed" et al.	NIV, NAS, NKJ, RSV, NRS, LB, NC
Acts 17:22	CHG "Mars Hill" TO "Areopagus"	NIV, NAS, NKJ, RSV, NRS, NC

Acts 17:22	REM "super-stitious" TO "religious"	NIV, NAS, NKJ, RSV, NRS, LB, NC
Acts 17:26	REM "blood"	NIV, NAS, RSV, NRS, LB, NC
Acts 17:29	CHG "Godhead" TO "Divine Nature", "divine being"	NIV, NAS, NKJ, RSV, NRS, LB, NC
Acts 19:35	REM "worshipper"	NIV, NAS, NKJ, RSV, NRS, LB, NC
Acts 20:21	REM "Christ"	NIV, NRS, NC
Acts 20:24	REM "none of these things move me. . ."	NIV, NAS, RSV, NRS, LB, NC
Acts 20:25	REM "of God"	NIV, NAS, RSV, NRS, LB
Acts 23:9	REM "let us not fight against God"	NIV, NAS, RSV, NRS, LB, NC
Acts 24:7	REM ENTIRE VERSE	NIV, NAS, RSV, NRS, NC
Acts 24:14	CHG "heresy" TO "sect"	NIV, NAS, NKJ, RSV, NRS, LB
Acts 24:15	REM "of the dead" (Resurrection)	NIV, NAS, RSV, NRS, LB
Acts 28:16	REM 11 WORDS	NIV, NAS, RSV, NRS, LB, NC
Acts 28:29	REM ENTIRE VERSE	NIV, NAS, RSV, NRS, LB, NC
Romans 1:3	REM "Jesus Christ our Lord"	NIV, NAS, RSV, NRS
Romans 1:16	REM "of Christ" (gospel of Christ)	NIV, NAS, RSV, NRS, NC
Romans 1:18	CHG "hold the truth" TO "suppress the truth"	NIV, NAS, NKJ,

Romans 1:25	CHG "changed the truth" TO "exchanged the truth"	NIV, NAS, NKJ, RSV, NRS, LB, NC
Romans 1:29	REM "fornication"	NIV, NAS, NKJ, RSV, NRS, LB, NC
Romans 5:8	CHG "commendeth" TO "demonstrates", et al.	NIV, NAS, NKJ, RSV, NRS, LB, NC
Romans 6:8	CHG "we be dead" TO "we died"	NIV, NAS, NKJ, RSV, NRS, LB, NC
Romans 6:11	REM "our Lord"	NIV, NAS, RSV, NRS, NC
Romans 8:1	REM LAST 10 WORDS	NIV, NAS, RSV, NRS, LB, NC
Romans 9:28	REM "in righteousness"	NIV, NAS, RSV, NRS, LB, NC
Romans 10:15	REM LAST 9 WORDS	NIV, NAS, RSV, NRS, LB, NC
Romans 10:17	CHG "word of God" TO "word of Christ"	NIV, NAS, RSV, NRS, LB, NC
Romans 11:6	REM LAST 18 WORDS ARE OMITTED	NIV, NAS, RSV, NRS, LB, NC
Romans 13:2	CHG "damnation" TO "judgment" et al.	NIV, NAS, NKJ, RSV, NRS, LB, NC
Romans 13:9	REM "Thou shall not bear false witness"	NIV, NAS, RSV, NRS, LB, NC
Romans 14:6	REM 15 WORDS	NIV, NAS, RSV, NRS, LB, NC
Romans 14:10	CHG "the judgement seat of Christ" TO "God's judgment seat" et al.	NIV, NAS, RSV, NRS, LB, NC

Romans 14:21	REM "or is offended, or is made weak"	NIV, NAS, RSV, NRS, LB, NC
Romans 14:23	CHG "damned" TO "condemned"	NIV, NAS, NKJ, RSV, NRS, LB, NC
Romans 15:8	REM "Jesus"	NIV, NAS, RSV, NRS, NC
Romans 15:19	REM "of God"	NIV, NAS, RSV, LB, NC
Romans 15:29	REM "of the gospel"	NIV, NAS, RSV, NRS, LB, NC
Romans 16:18	CHG "good words and fair speeches" TO "smooth talk and flattery"	NIV, NAS, NKJ, RSV, NRS, LB, NC
Romans 16:24	REM ENTIRE VERSE	NIV, NAS, RSV, NRS, NC
I Corinthians 1:21	CHG "foolishness of preaching" TO "foolishness of the message preached"	NIV, NAS, NKJ, RSV, NRS, LB, NC
I Corinthians 1:22	REM "require" TO "request", "ask" (Jews require a sign)	NIV, NAS, NKJ, RSV, NRS, LB, NC
I Corinthians 5:4	REM "Christ" (TWICE)	NIV, NAS, RSV, NRS, LB, NC
I Corinthians 5:7	REM "for us" (Christ sacrificed)	NIV, NAS, RSV, NRS, NC
I Corinthians 6:9	CHG "effeminate" TO "male prosti-tutes" et al.	NIV, NAS, NKJ, RSV, NRS, LB, NC
I Corinthians 6:20	REM "and in your spirit, which are God's	NIV, NAS, RSV, NRS, NC
I Corinthians 7:5	REM "fasting" (with prayer)	NIV, NAS, RSV, NRS, LB, NC

I Corinthians 7:39	REM "by the law" (The wife is bound)	NIV, NAS, RSV, NRS, LB, NC
I Corinthians 9:1	REM "Christ"	NIV, NAS, RSV, NRS, LB, NC
I Corinthians 9:27	CHG "I keep my body" TO "I beat my body" et al.	NIV, NAS, RSV, NRS, LB, NC
I Corinthians 9:27	CHG "castaway" TO "disquali- fied" et al.	NIV, NAS, NKJ, RSV, NRS, LB, NC
I Corinthians 10:28	REM LAST 10 WORDS ("the earth is the Lord's. . .")	NIV, NAS, RSV, NRS, LB, NC
I Corinthians 11:11	REM "in the Lord"	NIV, NAS, RSV, NRS, LB, NC
I Corinthians 11:24	REM "take eat. . . broken. . ." (Lord's Supper)	NIV, NAS, RSV, NRS, LB, NC
I Corinthians 11:29	CHG "damnation" TO "judgment" (Lord s Supper)	NIV, NAS, NKJ, RSV, NRS, LB, NC
I Corinthians 11:29	REM "unworthily"	NIV, NAS, RSV, NRS, NC
I Corinthians 14:33	CHG "author of confusion" TO "a God of disorder" et al.	NIV, NAS, RSV, NRS, LB, NC
I Corinthians 15:47	CHG "Lord from heaven" TO "man from heaven"	NIV, NAS, RSV, NRS, LB, NC
I Corinthians 15:55	CHG "grave" TO "Hades", "death"	NIV, NAS, NKJ, RSV, NRS, LB, NC
I Corinthians 16:22	REM "Jesus Christ"	NIV, NAS, RSV, NRS, LB, NC
I Corinthians 16:23	REM "Christ"	NIV, NAS, RSV, NRS, LB, NC

2 Corinthians 2:10	CHG "person of Christ" TO "presence of Christ"	NIV, NAS, NKJ, RSV, NRS, LB, NC
2 Corinthians 2:17	CHG "corrupt" TO "peddle", "sell" (word of God)	NIV, NAS, NKJ, RSV, NRS, LB, NC
2 Corinthians4:6	REM "Jesus"	NIV, NAS, RSV, LB, NC
2 Corinthians 4:10	REM "the Lord"	NIV, NAS, RSV, NRS, LB, NC
2 Corinthians 5:17	CHG "creature" TO "creation"	NIV, NAS, NKJ, RSV, NRS, LB, NC
2 Corinthians 5:18	REM "Jesus"	NIV, NAS, RSV, NRS, NC
2 Corinthians10:5	CHG "Casting down imaginations" TO "We demolish arguments" et al.	NIV, NAS, NKJ, RSV, NRS, LB, NC
2 Corinthians11:6	CHG "rude in speech" TO "untrained in speech"	NIV, NAS, NKJ, RSV, NRS, LB, NC
2 Corinthians11:31	REM "Christ"	NIV, NAS, RSV, NRS
Galatians 2:20	REM "nevertheless I live"	NIV, NAS, NKJ, RSV, NRS, LB, NC
Galatians 3:1	REM "that ye should not obey the truth"	NIV, NAS, RSV, NRS, LB, NC
Galatians3:17	REM "in Christ" (confirmed. . .of God in Christ)	NIV, NAS, RSV, NRS, LB, NC
Galatians 4:7	REM "through Christ" (heir of God through Christ)	NIV, NAS, RSV, NRS, LB, NC

Galatians 5:4	CHG "no effect" TO "estranged from", "alienated"	NIV, NAS, NKJ, RSV, NRS, LB, NC
Galatians 6:15	REM "For in Christ Jesus"	NIV, NAS, RSV, NRS, LB, NC
Galatians 6:17	REM "the Lord"	NIV, NAS, RSV, NRS, LB, NC
Ephesians 1:6	REM "accepted in the beloved"	NIV, NAS, RSV, NRS, LB, NC
Ephesians 3:9	REM "by Jesus Christ" (who created all things by)	NIV, NAS, RSV, NRS, LB, NC
Ephesians 3:14	REM "of our Lord Jesus Christ"	NIV, NAS, RSV, NRS, LB, NC
Ephesians 5:9	CHG "fruit of the Spirit" TO "fruit of the light"	NIV, NAS, RSV, NRS, LB, NC
Ephesians 5:30	REM "of his flesh, and of his bones"	NIV, NAS, RSV, NRS, LB, NC
Philippians 2:6	CHG "thought it not robbery to be equal with God" TO "did not consider equality with God something to be grasped" et al.	NIV, NAS, NKJ, RSV, NRS, LB, NC
Philippians 2:7	CHG "made" TO "emptied"	NAS, RSV, NRS, LB,
Philippians 3:8	CHG "dung" TO "rubbish", "trash"	NIV, NAS, NKJ, RSV, NRS, LB, NC
Philippians 3:16	REM LAST 13 WORDS	NIV, NAS, RSV, NRS, LB, NC
Philippians 4:13	CHG "through Christ" TO "through him"	NIV, NAS, RSV, NRS
Colossians 1:2	REM "and the Lord Jesus Christ"	NIV, NAS, RSV, NRS, LB, NC

Colossians 1:14	REM "through His blood" (redemption through. . .)	NIV, NAS, RSV, NRS, NC
Colossians 1:28	REM "Jesus"	NIV, NAS, RSV, NRS, LB, NC
Colossians 3:6	REM "on the children of disobedience"	NIV, NAS, RSV, LB, NC
1 Thessalonians 1:1	REM LAST 9 WORDS (from God our father. . .)	NIV, NAS, RSV, NRS, LB, NC
1 Thessalonians 2:19	REM "Christ"	NIV, NAS, RSV, NRS
1 Thessalonians 3:11	REM "Christ"	NIV, NAS, RSV, NRS, LB, NC
1 Thessalonians 3:13	REM "Christ"	NIV, NAS, RSV, NRS, LB, NC
1 Thessalonians 5:22	CHG "all appearance of evil" TO "every form of evil"	NIV, NAS, NKJ, RSV, NRS, LB, NC
2 Thessalonians 1:8	REM "Christ"	NIV, NAS, RSV, NRS
2 Thessalonians 1:12	REM "Christ"	NIV, NAS, RSV, NRS
1 Timothy 1:1	REM "Lord"	NIV, NAS, RSV, NRS, NC
1 Timothy 1:17	REM "wise" (the only wise God)	NIV, NAS, RSV, NRS, LB, NC
1 Timothy 2:7	REM "in Christ" (. . .the truth in Christ)	NIV, NAS, RSV, NRS, LB, NC
1 Timothy 3:16	CHG "God" TO "he" (God manifest in the flesh)	NIV, NAS, RSV, NRS, LB, NC
1 Timothy 4:12	REM "in spirit"	NIV, NAS, RSV, NRS, LB, NC

1 Timothy 5:21	REM "Lord"	NIV, NAS, RSV, NRS, NC
1 Timothy 6:1	CHG "blasphemed" TO "spoken against" et al.	NIV, NAS, RSV, LB, NC
1 Timothy 6:5	CHG "gain is god-liness" TO "godli-ness is a means of gain" et al.	NIV, NAS, NKJ, RSV, NRS, LB, NC
1 Timothy 6:5	REM "from such withdraw thyself"	NIV, NAS, RSV, NRS, NC
1 Timothy 6:10	CHG "root of all evil" TO "root of all kinds of evil"	NIV, NAS, NKJ, RSV, NRS, LB, NC
1 Timothy 6:19	CHG "eternal life" TO "the life that is truly life"	NIV, NAS, RSV, NRS, LB, NC
1 Timothy 6:20	CHG "science" TO "knowledge"	NIV, NAS, NKJ, RSV, NRS, LB, NC
2 Timothy 1:11	REM "of the gentiles"	NIV, NAS, RSV, NRS, NC
2 Timothy 2:15	REM "study" (only command to study the word)	NIV, NAS, NKJ, RSV, NRS, LB, NC
2 Timothy 3:3	CHG "of those that are good" TO "good"	NIV, NAS, NKJ, RSV, NRS, NC
2 Timothy 4:1	REM "the Lord"	NIV, NAS, RSV, NRS, LB, NC
2 Timothy 4:22	REM "Jesus Christ"	NIV, NAS, RSV, NRS, NC
Hebrews 1:3	CHG "by himself purged our sins" TO "provided puri-fication for sins"	NIV, NAS, RSV, NRS, NC

Hebrews 2:7	REM LAST 10 WORDS (and didst set him over the works. . .)	NIV, NAS, RSV, NRS, LB, NC
Hebrews 3:1	REM "Christ Jesus" (High Priest of our. . .)	NIV, NAS, RSV, NRS, LB, NC
Hebrews 7:21	REM "after the order of Melchisedec"	NIV, NAS, RSV, NRS, NC
Hebrews 10:34	REM "in heaven" (ye have in heaven a better)	NIV, NAS, RSV, NRS, NC
Hebrews 11:11	REM "was delivered of a child"	NIV, NAS, RSV, NRS, LB, NC
James 5:16	CHG "faults" TO "sins"	NIV, NAS, RSV, NRS, NC
1 Peter 1:22	REM "through the Spirit"	NIV, NAS, RSV, NRS, LB, NC
1 Peter 2:2	REM "of the word" (sincere milk of the word)	NIV, NAS, RSV, NRS, LB, NC
1 Peter 2:2	CHG "grow thereby" TO "grow up in your salvation"	NIV, NAS, RSV, NRS, LB, NC
1 Peter 3:15	CHG "the Lord God" TO "Christ as Lord" et al.	NIV, NAS, RSV, NRS, LB, NC
1 Peter 4:1	REM "for us" (Christ hath suffered for us)	NIV, NAS, RSV, NRS, LB, NC
1 Peter 4:14	REM LAST 15 WORDS	NIV, NAS, RSV, NRS, LB, NC
1 Peter 5:10	REM "Jesus"	NIV, NAS, RSV, NRS, LB, NC

1 Peter 5:11	REM "glory" (to Him be glory and dominion)	NIV, NAS, RSV, NRS, LB, NC
1 Peter 5:14	REM "Jesus"	NIV, NAS, RSV, NRS, LB, NC
2 Peter 2:1	CHG "damnable" TO "destructive"	NIV, NAS, NKJ, RSV, NRS, LB, NC
2 Peter 2:17	REM "for ever" (darkness is reserved for ever)	NIV, NAS, RSV, NRS, LB, NC
2 Peter 3:9	REM "us" TO "you"	NIV, NAS, RSV, NRS, LB, NC
1 John 1:7	REM "Christ"	NIV, NAS, RSV, NRS, LB, NC
1 John 3:16	REM "of God" (love of God)	NIV, NAS, NKJ, RSV, NRS, LB, NC
1 John 4:3	REM "Christ is come in the flesh" (antichrist)	NIV, NAS, RSV, NRS, LB, NC
1 John 4:9	REM "begotten"	NIV, NAS, RSV, NRS, LB, NC
1 John 4:19	REM "him" (We love him, because he first. . .)	NIV, NAS, RSV, NRS, LB, NC
1 John 5:7	REM LAST 15 WORDS	NIV, NAS, RSV, NRS, LB, NC
1 John 5:8	REM FIRST 9 WORDS	NIV, NAS, RSV, NRS, LB, NC
1 John 5:13	REM LAST 13 WORDS	NIV, NAS, RSV, NRS, LB, NC
1 John 5:13	ADD "continue to" (denies eternal security)	NKJ
2 John 1:3	REM "the Lord"	NIV, NAS, RSV, NRS, LB, NC
Jude 1:25	REM "wise" (Referring to God)	NIV, NAS, RSV, NRS, LB, NC

Revelation 1:8	REM "the beginning and the ending"	NIV, NAS, RSV, NRS, NC
Revelation 1:9	REM "Christ" (TWICE)	NIV, NAS, RSV, NRS, LB, NC
Revelation 1:11	REM "I am Alpha and Omega, the first and the last."	NIV, NAS, RSV, NRS, NC
Revelation 1:18	REM "hell"	NIV, NAS, NKJ, RSV, NRS, NC
Revelation 2:13	CHG "The satan's seat" TO "The satan's throne"	NIV, NAS, NKJ, RSV, NRS, LB, NC
Revelation 2:15	REM "which thing I hate"	NIV, NAS, RSV, NRS, LB, NC
Revelation 5:14	REM "Him that liveth for ever and ever"	NIV, NAS, RSV, NRS, LB, NC
Revelation 6:8	REM "Hell"	NIV, NAS, NKJ, RSV, NRS, NC
Revelation 6:17	CHG "his wrath" TO "their wrath"	NIV, NAS, RSV, NRS, LB, NC
Revelation 8:13	CHG "angel" TO "eagle"	NIV, NAS, RSV, NRS, LB, NC
Revelation 11:15	CHG "kingdoms" TO "kingdom"	NIV, NAS, RSV, NRS, LB, NC
Revelation 11:17	REM "and art to come"	NIV, NAS, RSV, NRS, LB, NC
Revelation 12:12	REM "inhabiters of"	NIV, NAS, RSV, NRS, NC
Revelation 12:17	REM "Christ"	NIV, NAS, RSV, NRS, LB, NC
Revelation 14:5	REM "before the throne of God"	NIV, NAS, RSV, NRS, LB, NC
Revelation 15:3	CHG "King of saints" TO "King of the ages" et al.	NIV, NAS, RSV, NRS, LB, NC

Revelation 16:5	REM "and shalt be" (refers to deity of Jesus)	NIV, NAS, RSV, NRS, LB, NC
Revelation 16:7	CHG "And I heard another out of the altar say" TO "And I heard the altar respond"	NIV, NAS, RSV, NRS
Revelation 16:17	REM "of heaven"	NIV, NAS, RSV, NRS, NC
Revelation 20:9	REM "from God out of"	NIV, NAS, RSV, NRS, NC
Revelation 20:12	CHG "God" TO "throne"	NIV, NAS, RSV, NRS, NC
Revelation 20:13	REM "hell"	NIV, NAS, NKJ, RSV, NRS, LB, NC
Revelation 20:14	REM "hell"	NIV, NAS, NKJ, RSV, NRS, NC
Revelation 21:24	REM "of them which are saved"	NIV, NAS, RSV, NRS, LB, NC
Revelation 22:14	CHG "do his commandments" TO "wash their robes"	NIV, NAS, RSV, NRS, LB, NC
Revelation 22:21	REM "Christ"	NIV, NAS, RSV, NRS, NC

About the Author

I an and Denise Foyn were called as Missionaries, by the Lord, to Taiwan where they had a profound effect on the locals in calling them to hear and obey the Voice of the Lord. Then, they were called to Lesotho where they ran a very successful Bible School. In New Zealand, they ministered to children and handicapped folk by means of puppets, illusion and other visual tools for evangelism. Family matters moved them to the UK where this book was completed. Ian's heart lies primarily in Evangelism and teaching others to do the same. As with Abram, Ian is called to follow the Lord "not knowing" [the where's or why's], he is to "only obey" (Genesis 12:1).

Ian and Denise have three children, all of whom are saints in their own right, and eleven Grandchildren with one *step* Granddaughter. In Lesotho, they gained more children and grandchildren from among their students by the love and care they demonstrated towards the local Saints. Their children and grandchildren are resident on three continents (New Zealand, Australasia; South Africa, Africa; United Kingdom, Europe.).

Ian accepted the Lord's invitation to eternal life on Easter Sunday, in 1969, and was filled with the Holy Spirit two years later. Since that day, and from the time he was told that he had just had a "spiritual experience and it will soon wear off," he has not been the same. Rather, he found that obeying the Lord has not worn off as promised by man, he has become more radical and dedicated than even he thought possible.

Lightning Source UK Ltd.
Milton Keynes UK
UKOW05f0823081213

222588UK00001B/17/P